My Little Book of Verse

Also by Jack Stanfield

America's Founding Fathers, Who are They?
We the Judges, Trampling the Constitution
Modernity, A World of Confusion: Causes
Modernity, A World of Confusion: Effects

My Little Book of Verse

by
Jack Stanfield

My Little Book of Verse

Order this book online at www.trafford.com
or email orders@trafford.com

Most Trafford titles are also available at major online book retailers.

Printed in Victoria, BC, Canada.

ISBN: 978-1-4269-2290-9

*Our mission is to efficiently provide the world's finest, most comprehensive
book publishing service, enabling every author to experience success.
To find out how to publish your book, your way, and have it available
worldwide, visit us online at www.trafford.com*

Trafford rev. 1/25/2010

Trafford PUBLISHING® www.trafford.com

North America & international
toll-free: 1 888 232 4444 (USA & Canada)
phone: 250 383 6864 ♦ fax: 812 355 4082

To my wife, Barbara

Table of Contents

Part I
Miscellany

Introduction

This little book of verse expresses my thoughts and feelings on the world of today. I have pulled together some previous poems created when traveling with the Corpus Christi Classics for their remembrance of the trip. I augmented these with poems on space and time, arts and science, modern culture, and religion. Some of these express pathos and lamenting over the state of modern society and Christianity, which seems to have lost its first century zeal. I hope you find something enjoyable or thought provoking in my fledgling attempt at verse. I divided the book into two parts: miscellany and an epic poem highlighting the amazing story of the people of God.

Arts and Science

The Universe

Is matter the universe;
Can we say for sure?
Mass-energy, nothing more,
Reality forever obscure?

There's quarks and atoms,
Particles and waves
That stay incognito,
Hide and seek their way.

Doing electrifying dances,
In energy conserving sway,
Immersed in a Higgs field,
Virtual particles arise to play.

A wave function guiding,
Uncertain, like a ghost,
Yet actual solids arise
 From possibilities' host.

Is this weirdness it?
What of the soul and the hope
Of rising at God's command;
Of eternity, man's vision scope?

Does nothingness win?
Life wasted on desires,
Despair and fading dreams,
Only entropy's disorder sired?

Master the immaterial,
For matter and spirit we are;
God's image inheritance
Reflected, thou somewhat marred.

The tangible universe is lacking,
For we think and have free will,
Showing duty and neighborly love;
Free agents, we're Spirit filled.

Seek wider wisdom,
God's love embrace;
Humbly serve others, and
Make earth a loving place.

Time

What is time, does anyone know:
Objectively or subjectively formed?
Continuous, discrete, does it stretch?
When was it actually born?

When did time first begin,
And will there be an ending?
Does it flow like a stream,
Or tick like a clock, bending?

In a flash, the universe appeared,
A Big Bang left it quaking,
With time arriving shortly after,
A case, they say, of symmetry breaking.

Is it senseless to speak of time
Being before, as the only thing existing
Was God's mind, which created
A universe that's still persisting?

Has time physical properties
Or is it only a measure of change?
Can we know its real essence
Through observations precisely gained?

Unlike a quality of space,
We can't select a time to be,
For we occupy all of time
At the place we chance to see.

For science, time is but a clock's tick,
For us humans, it's always flowing;
One gives a number and allows dilation,
The other, a river that's ongoing.

Like a log floating in a stream,
Our time runs down and out,
As nature's laws take their toll,
And the Grim Reaper lurks about.

Did time only begin with man,
Who observed it with his reason?
Time ceases for each man, it's true,
And all things in their season.

Trapped in time and space is our lot,
Aging and slowly dying each day,
For we're mortal, are we not,
Running up a bill we'll have to pay?

Time is an illusion, forever past,
As light-speed delays signals' reception,
Our brain and senses always catching up,
While the future is for us a mere projection.

Our soul straddles time and space;
A part in time and a part in eternity,
Timeless, united with our mortal body;
Yet, for the irreligious, that's an absurdity.

But something awaits us—no doubt.
As our time moves onward and out;
Some see death as nothing to relish,
But, to others, it's eternity that counts,
(As we enter into everlasting day.)

So we have no time to waste.
We live as each moment begins,
Fleeting and speeding by with
No delay, until all our moments end.

Space

Space behaves like a flexible fabric;
Its twisting and contorting abound
As matter and energy play a tune
That guides the stars around.

It surrounds objects everywhere
And invades us through and through;
Even the quarks can't escape
And are enveloped in her glue.

Her phantom-like qualities
Never come into our sight
As she swirls around all things,
Silently controlling their flight.

Expanding like a balloon,
She rushes away from her source,
Carrying all along in nature's way,
On a yet uncharted future course.

Where is she expanding into
Is unknowable to us now;
For she could be flat or enclosed,
Her contents ultimately deciding how.

But space remains an enigma:
If mass and energy go poof,
Only she would be left,
A quiet thing, her life aloof.

Space is yet little understood
As to her essence, to be sure—
She, only mathematical formulae,
A gossamer substance, but secure.

She displays her geometrical side
In the form of metric tensors,
Which express her personality,
Observed through man-made sensors.

But it is said by some conjurors,
Who are enamored of her nature to tell,
That she becomes chaotic in her demeanor,
If she's confined to a Planck-sized cell.

Yet all of this is pure speculation,
As she hides her mysteries very well,
Being of a sensitive nature,
Prying into her reality often fails.

Life is "Quarky"

Some say that life is quirky,
And for many that is true,
But for me, it becomes "quarky,"
The more science I pursue.

As I wind through the maze
Of solids, molecules, and atoms,
Protons, mesons, and hadrons,
I find quarks lurking there as phantoms.

Making up all things that abound,
Strange creatures never mapped,
Illusive and foreign to most,
Requiring clever tools to entrap.

Their behavior and properties
Leave us dubious and short of wind,
Hopping from top, flavors, and spin,
With assorted colors that blend.

Confined in time, all dressed in white,
They came together with a din
To make a world of countless particles,
Force taking mass for a spin.

Quarky creatures are now a sensation,
As they enliven and light the world,
Forming the elements on which it rests,
As their electrifying dance unfurls.

We live in a quarky world, for sure,
As I pound on a desk composed
Mostly of air and elements rare,
While virtual particles come and go.

Where has my solid world gone,
As it dissolves in evanescence,
Melting away with deeper probing
To bring us closer to our very essence?

But this image little satisfies my longing;
My heart seeks its very source,
With its substance insubstantial,
Yet containing my very self, of course.

Confusing me is another possibility
That is born of scientific scorn,
Thin strings playing various notes,
The world becoming a musical score.

Thus the weight on your shoulders
Comes from an explicit repeated note;
Played around the expanding universe,
Until the melody formed became rote.

Is it any wonder I'm so confused
When told spirits can't exist?
Yet of quarky things and many strings,
One seldom, if ever, balks or resists.

Is all of this just an illusion
Based on models from here and there?
Emerging from man's enlarging pride,
In the end, is man left stranded here?

Yet there is an eternity waiting
If we but seek an expanded guide;
Accept the presence of the supernatural,
The true source of the universe's pride.

Beauty and Truth Dismissed

God is beauty, goodness, and truth
That our human nature seeks to find,
Savoring the surprise that beauty excites,
That transcends the strictly animal kind.

In beauty, we elevate ourselves on high,
Above our lowly profane existence,
To soar with the angel's heavenly delights—
Our soul claims a part of eternity's persistence.

It is the things thought beautiful by us
That inspire us to increase their splendor,
As great cathedrals climb into the heavens,
To God's beauty and wonder, they surrender.

These magnificent structures and classical art
Please the senses and the heart uplift,
Still bring joy, reflecting life's goodness,
And to the people of God, a profound gift.

Even the pagans understood the wonder
Of the gods' domain and its universality,
Erecting structures of beauty and wonder
To escape life's drudgery and perversity.

Yet in these modern times called progressive,
Art and structures have no beauty to portray;
All is increasingly profane, ugliness prevails,
As modern man's view of himself is on display.

The dynamism of the cave paintings amazed,
And art of the Middle Ages its beauty conveyed,
But modern art is deplorable by contrast,
With all aesthetic beauty openly depraved.

For progressive man seeks not life but death;
His world unbearable, with nothingness his end.
Nihilism is his guide, leaving him a forlorn slave
To addictions and afflictions, not able to fend.

His music is of a similar tenor as well,
Uttering hauntingly his angst and bitter plight;
In his corruption, his soul in sore distress,
A world lacking purpose to give his spirit flight.

His is to seek the God of beauty and goodness,
If he's to escape from despair and death's grip;
For, there, joy and abundant life is to be found
Among God's people, into despair no more to slip.

Oh, Deer!

The deer frolic and play
Around my garden every day.
In the spring the fawns
Are seen all spotted on my lawn.
Tiny things springing around,
As mother chews her cud aground.
They wander not too far away,
Exploring nature as a sort of play.
It's a wonder to watch them grow,
As their mother slowly lets them go.

In the fall, I gather more facts,
Seeing the males' glorious racks.
The larger ones sun in the yard,
Keeping their space, yearlings apart.
They're an engaging sort, racks hooking,
As I stand in amazement, looking.
They wander off to the forest near
To start the cycle of life for next year.

By the dozens they come and go,
Destroying all thoughts of flowers to grow.
Lazily laying, chewing in the shade,
As I watch forlornly my disappearing blades.
Yet I can't complain too much.
Their antics delight, with joy I'm touched.
I watch a fawn's toe tap my deck twice,
As it echo's back to him, sounding nice.

So let them come in a bunch
To munch on my grass for their lunch.
I'll yell at them now and then,
If on the bushes they chew again.
This contact brings me a sort of wisdom,
As all life abounds in God's kingdom.

Spring Snow

A storm gathers during the day,
As the clouds shift, turning gray.
There is lightning and thunder,
Rain, hail, and snow, a wonder.
Bands of snow, heavy at times,
As nature powders the swaying pines.
Animals vanish from the scene,
Awaiting the sun, earth made clean.
Wind is up and the snow blown,
Creating sculptures no one owns.
Sun comes out, the snow escapes,
The earth an enlivened landscape.
Spring flowers spout and bloom,
Earth, colored, dispelling winter's gloom.

Travel

O' Johnny Boy
(To our Welsh bus driver)

O' Johnny boy, the wheels, the wheels are rolling,
From glen to glen and cross the mountains high;
For it is you that must drive so we can safely ride.
And come ye through the narrow country road,
Or by the river wide,
We were there with you, o' Johnny boy,
In rain and often sunny times.
And, when, for those lovely English shores
We will again pine,
We'll think of you, o' Johnny boy,
With fondness and good cheer;
And, proudly, once more raise a tribute to you,
With a glass of good ol' English beer.

Niagara Falls

Do you know the way to Niagara Falls?
I've never been there at all.
I don't know the way.
Can I get there from Philadelphia, PA?
And should I go the scenic byway,
Or by the much faster highway?

Do you know the way to Niagara Falls?
They say the falls are big and tall!
Do you know the way to Buffalo?
They say it's on the way—is that okay?

Do you know the way to Niagara Falls?
I yearn to hear the river's singing call.
I heard it ends on the road called Rainbow,
So is that the way I should go?
If I cross the bridge and follow Queen's Way
Will I see the river flowing to the falls today?

Do you know the way to Niagara Falls?
They say they're for young and old, short and tall.
Will the Maid of the Mist get me there,
If I wear the proper all-weather gear?
It's in my sights—I hear a roaring serenade,
Flowing unceasingly, water on parade.

A Friendly Holiday

Day 1: All Aboard

The weather was crisp and bright;
A rowdy crowd boarded the bus with delight.
Roger and Kathy and Fred and Bev
Soon got us organized and presently fed.
We rambled over the Kansas prairies flat,
To Montana Mike's to partake of a flavorful repast.
As hale and hardy a bunch as you ever did see,
Then traveled onward to the city of Abilene.
The day ended with a feast fulfilled,
Compliments of the staff at the Brookville Hotel.

Day 2: A Brief Excursion

The old folks were nestled in bed lying prone,
When their dreams were shattered
   by the clatter of the phone.
They climbed into the coach in anticipation
Of a day full of fun and relaxation.
The Crown Center visit gave a Hallmark insight,
Then food, shopping, and motel rest,
   before embracing the night.
The Ameristar casino gave sights, sounds,
   nourishment, and gambler's remorse,
Followed by Roger's colorful discourse.

Day 3: An Animal Show

A leisurely departure—to Cabella's sport emporium
  we went,
Seeing displays of animals awesomely set,
  quite an unusual event.
With elephants, lions, tigers, fish, mountain goats,
  and such
So handsomely mounted were to our senses
  almost too much.
Food and drink and rambling away to Branson,
Once there to see the Christmas lights most handsome.
To bed and perchance to dream
Of things anticipated, yet unseen.

Day 4: Let the Shows Begin

After a breakfast of light and casual fare,
We traveled to a village grand without a care.
With browsing and lunch and a little more joe,
It was off to see our very first show.
The entertainers O'Donnell and Duff
Sang Irish songs; with Danny Boy, I was touched.
Traditional Christmas carols were fine indeed,
With Barbara and Millie immortalized on DVDs.
Our second show had talent aplenty,
A mixture of lights and sounds that enchanted many.
From a virtuoso who handled multiple keyboards
    that surprised,
To violinist, guitarist, and drummer, who kept us
  all energized.

Day 5: A Fitting End

With a holy beginning that gathered us to church
  one and all,
Then on to that redundantly named restaurant,
  "Shorty Smalls."
A circuitous route to a turnout, a river valley to see,

Ultimately brought us to Smirnoff—Yakov,
  that would be.
He filled the bill by giving us a laugh or two,
A quirky sense of humor and jokes that were new.
A final spectacular extravaganza that only Shoji
  could provide,
Let us end the day on a bit of a high.
Penguins waddling around and deer in grass skirts
   were a sight
That left us giggling and laughing with delight.
Shoji's violin and music selection
Ran the gambit from Big Band, western, and
  some classical, I detected.
'Twas a fitting climax to our stay in Branson,
  you bet,
Made possible by those classics, Fred and Bev,
  who got it all set.
So let's give them—Roger and Kathy, too—
  a big hand,
For they did a great job getting us here,
  as they stuck to their original plan.

Like the priest at Mass said, be good,
  be brief, be gone;
Since I'm not the first two, I'll just END.

A Mackinac Adventure
(AKA, the Old Folks Still Play)

Day 1

To start this poem, all I can say is, "What the heck,
We're on a new adventure with Kathy Dec!"
The assemblage arrived early on,
As we drove to Denver at the crack of dawn.
There were lots of familiar and some new faces,

Looking to enjoy the exploration of new places.
Flying to Chi Town, we coached to Grand Rapids,
Day one left us somewhat tried, but primed for action.

Day 2

In the morning, after some filling and milling,
It was off to absorb the Dutch, and all were willing.
A clear morning to the Dutch Village we went,
To see sights of the Old World transferred hence.
With organs and high-stepping dancers whose
  wooden shoes click-clacked,
Stores to shop for Delft and Dutch stuff,
  our time passed fast.
Then off to Holland, a city quite quaint,
To lunch, shop, meander, but not to be late.
We're due at Windmill Island to assess,
A 247-year-old windmill and the only certified
  woman miller in the Midwest.
Six stories up we climbed, an authentically
  dressed maiden doing her spiel,
Of how it was transplanted to mill grain,
  all its parts quite real.
Then to church, with a cracker-jack priest teaching,
Gave Barb and I a blessing for fifty years
  Of marriage reaching.
At the end of the day, one could reasonably trust
The group was thoroughly in touch with the Dutch.

Day 3

The next morning it was scenery and the water's way,
At Sault St. Marie, the rapids came to play.
Traveling north with luscious landscape scene,
We were enthralled with the copious amount of green.
The Soo Locks experience was fascinating by boat,
As we went from low to high, narrated by our host.
The travel was smooth, the explanation clear,
Learning the lock's history, we boated with good cheer.

Then at the hotel, we were on our own,
Some to casinos and some stayed home.

Day 4

This morning our hearts gave a lift,
   our object afore,
As we were ferried to Mackinac Island,
   once all were safely aboard.
On arriving at this famous island quaint,
A narrated tour by horse-drawn carriage awaited.
Then it was off to explore the place
   where cars were forgot,
Enjoying the beautiful trees of lilacs,
   so sweet and easy to spot.
Many indulged in the famous fudge,
   delicious, I'd say,
As we explored the town's shops
   and entertaining ways.
And the horse-drawn carriage rides we found
Passed an aroma around,
   and left large deposits on the ground.
At the end of the day, all were tired,
   yet happy and tranquil,
Anticipating the Grand Hotel
   and an elegant lunch that fills.

Day 5

The morning showed cloudy with a chance of rain,
Conditions yet reasonable to explore, with new
      experiences to gain.
Off to the Villa de Lac tour, with imagining and facts,
A Victorian-cottage setting that projected us back.
Then we horsed to the Grand Hotel for lunch,
Where we entered a different time
   of the grand and opulence.
From the Grand's large porch one sees
   a manicured park of tranquility,

With fountain, lilacs, and horse topiary
   a restful part of the facility.
The rain and cold could ne'r deter the hardy ones,
Who, despite the weather, continued their fun.
The traditional party hosted by Fred and Bev once again
Drew a crowd of congenial imbibers and friends.
As the day ends, there is a feeling of sadness
   for leaving this place,
That evoked a sense of order, calmness,
   and a rejuvenating pace.

Day 6

This morning we leave this unique idea
   of gracious living,
To the mainland to be immersed in Bavaria
   without misgiving.
Some final shopping and a short jet-boat ride
   with its rooster's tail,
It was off to Mackinaw City we all did sail.
In parting, the Grand Hotel and Mackinac Bridge views
Left their images on our minds, as a remembrance
   of the magic we knew.
We rambled on to another place and another day,
Where we would again have a chance to play.

Day 7

Today, the Town of Frankenmuth gives us a touch
   of Germany most fair,
We absorb its architecture and the sight of flowers
   everywhere.
A tour of town and the 1846 Lutheran Church Lorenz,
The manicured lawns, covered bridge, a pleasant event.
One last chance at a shopping spree,
As we wandered around after being set free.
Then off to Bronner's Christmas Wonderland,
   a myriad of decorations,
That fills one's senses and instigates a sense

of anticipation.
This evening, we added to our weight—
    now long forgotten—when
We dined on fried chicken and all the fixin's
    at the Bavarian Inn.
What remains of the day we reflect on
    all we saw and did on this trip,
Knowing the time of frivolity with our friends
    has now by us slipped.
We prepare for our Chicago return
    and saying our farewells
To this fair company, and Kathy, Bev, and Fred,
    Who, once again, did not fail.

All hail the adventurous spirit of this merry crew,
May we gather once again a year hence, to begin anew!

A Canadian Rockies Holiday
    (AKA, An Epic Journey)

Day 1

Kathy, Sandi, and Falcon Tours showed the way
For our Canadian Rockies Holiday.
Like those intrepid explorers Abbott and Costello,
    Crosby and Hope,
We gathered together and boarded the coach.
Going north and west, the coach started to roll
With fun and games, Rock Springs our first goal.

Day 2

Next morning we arose: "To Jackson Hole!" we cry.
We made it by lunch, and a chance to buy, buy, buy!
At the Tetons, the Snake we found;
In groups of six, we floated the river down.

Eagles with babies we espied,
The flora and fauna pointed out by our guide.
We saw the Tetons, their grandeur late,
And understood why they were called great!

Day 3

On to Yellowstone Park roam we would;
The Tetons, enveloped in fog and clouds
  Where they stood
Mysteriously showing their beauty grand,
A wonder springing up from the surrounding land.

Yellowstone Park displayed its many surprises,
Elk, bear, pelican, and bison.
Nature in a state of change and renewal
Gave us a sense of her order and her rules.
Yellowstone Falls and geysers tall,
With Old Faithful entertaining us all.
Sandi the coach she maneuvered well
Around a tree in the road that fell,
And when exhausted by our fun,
We ended at the fly fishing capitol of the world:
  Livingston.

Day 4

Day Four started bright and clear.
From Livingston to Kalispell, Sandi steered.
Across Big Sky country the coach explored,
With all those inside wanting to see more.
And, as from Day One, using that word obscene (bus),
Twenty-five cents kept filling Kathy's Bandit machine.
In the midst of a state large comprised,
Kathy detoured and all were surprised.

The first ever Smokejumper Center we entered
  with trepidation,
As a means to enhance our education.

To hear a story of courage and dedication,
Of men and women fine and brave deserving
  of our ovation!
Who, in the face of fire, heat, and peril, stand tall;
A young handsome guide informs us all.
Then it's on to Kalispell, our night's destination,
Large, clear, and blue, Flathead Lake gives inspiration.

Day 5

Day Five finds us among Glacier Park's scenic wonders;
We board a magic "Red Bus" to be guided yonder.
Across the Garden Wall we climb high and east,
Weeping walls, valley deep, waterfalls,
  and skittish sheep.
Like bookends, Lakes McDonald and St. Mary's
  frame our time,
With spectacular views from the beginning of our climb.

O, Canada, you now call us across Alberta's flat prairies,
With everyone on board furiously eating their fresh cherries!
On this occasion, the shy "I'ma late-a" suddenly
  arises to play,
Giving cheers and laughter—quite a display.

Day 6

Early we rise to see Banff, then back to nature
To take a walk on the Athabasca Glacier.
In every trip some rain must fall down;
Today, from Banff, ours followed us around.
The mountain tops peeked in and out,
A misty, eerie scene to everyone, no doubt.
Aboard a "SnoCoach" a climb steep
So atop the Glacier we could reach.
All on board were willingly exposed
To nature's constantly moving compacted snow.
Returning to Banff via Lake Louise,
Its grandeur and prestige was sure to please.

Fairy Princes Millie gave us a laugh delight,
With wand, tiara, and glasses with wipers and lights.

Day 7

Stampede Day dawns clear, and on a lark,
We were off to visit Heritage Park.
Train, paddlewheel boat, and a town of old
Brought together for future generations to behold.
Next, to the Stampede grounds to discover and mingle
With "wannabe" cowpokes both married and single.
Caught on the Midway in a crowd walking cheek to cheek,
I tell you, boys, it was no place for the weak or the meek!

We gathered at the grandstands, up five stories,
A group eager for fun and to view contestants' glories.
We witnessed chuck wagon races, tough and gory,
Competing for a moment of fleeting glory.
After the dust settled, stage set, and no sign of rain,
We experienced a "spectacular" forever etched
    in our brains.
Young Canadians, native peoples, Olympians,
    acrobats, strongmen, and songs,
Entertained with energy, pace, and athletic feats
    as the show moved rapidly along.
A firework "extravaganza" coordinated from
    beginning to end with the show highlights,
Left us oohing and aahing with the final cannonade
    sounding like fiercely fought fights.

So a big ovation is owed to Sandi and Kathy Dec,
For they made possible and safe this wonderful trek!
And Fred and Bev, please do take a big bow,
For your untiring effort, the trip to allow.

Culture

"Newspeak"

In making a name for ourselves,
We've created a Tower of Babel.
Freely distorting words' meanings;
Understanding fails when speaking prattle.

Orwell's *1984* foresaw our demise:
"Newspeak," censorship, and rot
Enforced by political correctness—
No objective truth, wisdom long forgot.

Schools the implementing tool
For the elitist's world view,
Forgo free speech and reason
For propaganda and facts gone askew.

Meaning is purposely misconstrued:
Bad is good and good is bad,
Confusion reigns, skepticism ripe,
Evil abides in a world collectively mad.

Profanity and vulgarity unbridled,
With the younger set, often abused,
Giving their bodies up lightly—
No modesty left, anybody can use.

Religious speech publicly barred:
One's sensitivities might be ruffled,
Shame felt, or evil ways exposed,
Leaving righteous protest stifled.

With "texting" a dominate mode,
Decaying language skills frame
A world restricted in its wisdom,
As thought expression goes wan.

As America dumbs down
With fewer ideas prevalent,
Factions erupt, anger ignites,
True freedom becomes irrelevant.

Where Have All the Children Gone?

Where have all the children gone?
Many couples but children few,
Forgoing the hassle they demand,
Rejecting love's gift, the world askew.

Where have all the children gone?
To abortion clinics, body mush;
It's so easy to be rid of this thing,
There's no fuss, all's kept hush, hush.

A death wish is a modern's way,
As millions of babies die each year;
Sterile relations win the day,
Pleasure triumphs, virtue never near.

In prior times

Laughter at table and pungent fun,
With lots of scrapes and tears;
Life spontaneity shown, zest, joy:
Kids lacking today's suffocating fears.

In the family, life was learned:
Sharing, caring, getting along,
Bruised egos, fallen, yet standing tall,
Charity, all singing life's love song.

At Christmas, families gathered
Around the tree and greeting guest,
Uproarious fun and entertainment,
The church's celebration the best.

Family reunions gathered the clan,
Multitude of kids and cousins all,
Aunts and uncles, too, always present,
Good feelings, food, and a game of ball.

Currently

Eerily quiet in families everywhere,
As children are scorned.
Self-fulfillment's now the quest;
Joy, playfulness gone, life forlorn.

Children denied a childhood,
Not free to innocently explore and play,
Missing out on nature's treasures,
No longer found in pockets at close of day.

Plunked in front of TV or a game,
Made to act and look mature, a new fad,
Draining joy from too many,
As seen in eyes, old and sad.

Media grotesquely exhibits children,
Satisfying sadistic inner needs;
Nihilistic culture lacking shame,
Abortion spawns depravity's seeds.

Evil has arisen, children abused,
Pawns in parent's resentful games;
They're placed in harm's way
As domestic partners hurt and maim.

Where have all of the children gone?
Their ranks are rapidly thinning,

Couples rejecting God's co-creation plan;
Pleasure, not love, is daily winning.

With the state now raising kids,
Missing is discipline, nourishing love;
Given mere existence, childhood lost,
The Word left unspoken—enters the evil one.

Joining gangs, many addictions tried
For lack of attention, money failing to fill
The gaps in love missed, virtue lost,
Kids disrespecting, lives left unfulfilled.

Where have all the children gone?
A question now wrought in pain;
An inconvenience to women, they're
Aborted; neglect, abuse the new refrain.

*Father, forgive them; they do not
know what they are doing.* Luke 23:34

Sin of Scandal

*"Woe to the man through
    whom scandal comes."* Matthew 18:7

The smell of scandal
Is rancid, defusing in the air about,
Spreading among Christians,
Putting Christ's saving light out.

Politicians, teachers, leaders
Dismiss Christ in seeking fame
From what they say and do,
Disgracing His blessed name.

Sinning against Christ's words,
Their souls slowly shrivel up;
Life's everlasting day forfeited
For fleeting power that corrupts.

Clergy of all denominations
Similarly themselves deceive,
Saying sin is defined by men,
The Master's words not believed.

Millstone around the neck
Would be preferable to hell,
Damnation a high price
For fleeting power, one's soul to sell.

Those in authority sin gravely,
As their actions cause others to sin;
They're answerable to the Lord,
When their mortal life naturally ends.

"It would be better for anyone who
leads astray one of these little ones
who believes in me, to be drowned…"
Matthew 18:6

Clearly there are consequences
For the message one has sent
That's dismissed by many believers;
They could face agony, garments rent.

Return to Christ's teaching;
Humbly follow His way;
Be moral in your actions,
Holding all scandal at bay.

Time of Discontent

Economy falling,
Stock market dropped,
Trillions lost,
Expectations flip-flopped.

Unemployment climbing,
People hurting a lot,
Distress, disillusionment,
Foreclosures none can stop.

Bailouts of institutions,
Billions of stimulus funds,
Dems pay back their backers,
Progress, a select few to none.

States overextended,
Governments bloated,
Programs expanded,
Spending exploded.

Wants unrestrained,
Tax base depleted,
Freeloading thriving,
Revenues exceeded.

Hopes shattered,
Angst growing,
The frugal rebelling,
Angry at money owing.

Red ink, printed money,
Posterity's dreams crushed
Under rising debt load,
Silent majority un-hushed.

Capitalism at risk,
Socialism astir,
Future uncertain,
Can't stay as you were.

Take a stand,
Turn nation aright,
Throw scoundrels out,
Enter into the fight.

Sarah's All Grown Up!

Our granddaughter is quite the accomplished one,
All grown up, an architecture degree she has won.
But being a bright and committed student yet,
She seeks a higher degree in design to get.
She has always had her independent ways,
Focused energies, keeping her prize in her gaze.

As we think of Sarah with a love that binds,
A kaleidoscope of images flashes through our minds.
We see her small, wearing a lovely special dress,
A "twirling spotted" one, changing often to look her best.
Or the image, at three, wearing a dress with smocking
To pick blackberries in Mississippi, a bit shocking.
Or in a garden park holding Grandpa's hand,
So I'd see all the lovely flowers while in Spokane.
Other times we'd pick strawberries and cherries,
And we'd wolf them down, the family making merry.

With her mother and sister, she came a month to stay,
Greg on duty; at times, she'd vanish in a world away.
She went to a land existing only in her mind,
A place beyond our comprehension she'd go find.
In her rite of passage, she came to Colorado at ten—
Flew to visit grandparents, a joy shared with us then.

She listened to Grandpa spout baloney to impress her,
As we'd argued about the site in "Balonia" I inferred.

She took to riding horses and ballet lessons, too,
Gaining confidence and grace, learning something new.
She'd lovingly show her latest ballet steps to us,
So we could be a part of her life—for us a must.
Sports, boys, prom nights we'd not personally know
Except by Teresa keeping us appraised by video show.
Years fly by and we're at a school graduation scene;
Sarah grown, leaving the nest, still somewhat green

She is a self-assured person who knows her own mind;
Motivated, bright, knowing her wants at all times.
Good in math and science, challenging herself anew,
She selected architecture as her artistic talents she grew.
She excels at models, and the quality of her designs
Her professors impressed, all her grades just fine.
An overseas semester increased her artistic smarts,
As she sketched her way through Italy's magnificent classical art

Unbelievably, she's now graduating from Ames;
On to graduate school to enhance her skills
   and to garner some fame.
Life's open; in wonder we'll watch her blossom,
   as she keeps us guessing;
In all you do, Sarah, may you find happiness
   and Almighty God's blessing.
In pure love, we congratulate you, lovely Sarah,
Wishing you the best and shouting our hurrahs!

A takeoff of W.S. Gilbert's song, "I Am the Very Model of a Modern Major-General."

I Am the Very Image of a Modern Presidential

I've knowledge of image, packaging, and everything rhetorical
And I send ideas soaring euphorical as I quote all things
      lyrical,
From entitlements to post-racial relations, in order
      categorical.
I'm very well acquainted, too, with matters economical,
As I understand taxes simple, intricate, and astronomical.
And on other's wealth, I'm liberal with my suggestions;
With cheerful attacks, I inflict on the rich major indigestion.

All
With cheerful attacks, etc.

Prez
I'm proficient with Twitter and Facebook presentations,
I know the triggers that elicit feelings of adulation.
In short, in matters of image, packaging, and rhetorical,
I am the very image of a modern presidential.

All
In short, in matters of image, packaging, and rhetorical,
He is the very model of a modern presidential.

Prez
 I know philosophers from Karl Marx to Kierkegaard,
 And Sartre, Freud, Rand, Sanger and Mead, I regard,
 As the basis for my "Orwellian Newspeak" and my devotion
      to radical feminism,
And I can quote the tenets of liberalism and tout the joys
      of individualism.
In all situations, I glibly recite the value of relativism,
And extol, "Can't we just get along?" quoting tolerance's
      many abominable truisms.
I can identify a villain and thereby popularity with the
      masses gain,
And I'll promise anything my office to retain.

All
In short, he is the very image of a modern presidential.

Prez
 I can expound on any subject and seem quite precocious,
 And use a "teleprompter" so as not to sound atrocious.
 I can act a part and not seem ingenuous or hypocritical;
 In short, in matters of image, packaging, and rhetorical,
 I am the very image of a modern presidential.

All
In short, in matters of image, packaging, and rhetorical,
He is the very image of a modern presidential.

Prez
In short, when I know what's meant by honor and humility,
When I can obfuscate right, truth, and candor with facility,
When I can act like Alice's Tweedledum and Tweedledee,
To gain an advantage over my foes with "dexteritee,"
When I've learnt what's new in the application of flattery,
When I can invent nonsensical slogans to sell my rhetoric,
In short, when I've a smattering of experience, you see,
You'll say a better presidential has never been so at sea.

All
You'll say a better, etc.

Prez
For my executive experience, tho' I'm smart and plucky,
Has only been theoretical and negligible, yet I'm lucky;
Still in matters of image, packaging, and rhetorical,
I am the very image of a modern presidential

All
But still in matters of image, packaging, and rhetorical,
He is the very image of a modern presidential.

Dualism Unmasked: Who Am I?

(Dualism asserts that a human being is composed
of two separate substances: a material body
and an immaterial thinking mind.)

Dualism erupted as the Rational Age began,
With Descartes' "I think, therefore I am."
A thinking being arose separated from material man,
That is, by nature's law, not hers to command.

Descartes' fallacy was he forgot a basic fact:
That there first must be a being to think about,
More properly put: "I am, therefore I think," but, alas,
He made gods of mere men—"I AM!" they now gladly shout.

Descartes separated matter from self: two substances,
With a thinking part not compelled to act,
 But to choose a path without law's coercion;
An immaterial thing, ghostly, given all the facts.

The self has no apparent material nature present,
A thinking principle somehow not commingled.
A phantom, called mind, not in the flesh resident,
Not properly a being of the brain's electrical signals.

To Descartes, the self was a specter of the mind,
An intelligent thing separate from his body;
A replacement for the soul, in degree and in kind;
Not materialistic, it wasn't a scientific commodity.

(The soul is the form of the body, the primary
principle of life that is fulfilled when embodied.)

In today's irrational world, the soul no longer plays;
As the brain creates the mind, the self a mere illusion,
With genes the life-force forming a body that decays,
Leaving only matter behind, the soul an archaic delusion.

But don't we seem more than electrical currents,
As thoughts are ours, unless they're shared?
Thoughts arise in infinite variety when there's no deterrent,
Giving each life its richness of joy and despair.

So life's principle seems more than chemically forged,
As we can change the world based on pondered choice,
Dispelling the predestined rhetoric being disgorged
By science and philosophy, which materialism on us foist.

For we are conscious of things beyond us
That we can see and touch and smell,
Showing we're independent beings, who trust
In us to make our selections—we're not compelled!

The enigmatic soul remains a disquieting reality,
Explaining life, future destines, and man internally.
It is, it seems, the primary basis of our vitality,
Forming us and extending our being into eternity.

All beings have a natural form and traits
That the soul properly gives rise to,
Informing our structure, behavior and fate,
Yet, itself, immaterial, a mysterious glue.

It grants man the power to think, judge, and will,
Abstracting concepts from gathered images seen,
And creates the thoughts we think, wishes to fulfill,
Combines spirit and the fleshy powers we so esteem.

Scientific instruments have no facilities to see
How the soul's powers effect our bodily actions
That define our nature; thinking makes us free
To choose and change, selecting our own reactions.

Of the soul's great powers to direct our lives,
Consciousness is one of the results perceived
That allows us to conceive of our self, as derived
From images of the world that the intellect retrieves.

Thus the mind is but a power of the soul manifest
That conceives of thoughts and abstract beings,
Displaying the unity of a body and soul coalesced
That effect all its powers, the "compound I" we're seeing.

Life is known by its various activities exposed,
And so a primary principle of life is required;
Tho' not shown from the material to have arose,
One supposes another substance that lights life's fire.

This substance does the whole body drench,
In being before the human body itself exists.
Immaterial, God created and individually sent,
Forming and guiding growth so life persists.

Like yeast throughout dough is kneaded,
Or like the Higgs Field spread through space is received,
The soul encompasses all our parts, none deleted,
Its powers to think and will jointly conceived.

God gave man a co-creation power to propagate
His species; the fleshy material man does supply,
But existence comes from Him—some He delegates
To the soul that infuses the body, life to provide.

This subsistence substance, by its nature living
Beyond the fleshy body's duration, invites
Each to seek God's grace by love giving,
So happily reunited, a glorified body takes flight.

The body raised perfects the soul's inherent nature,
Adding powers lacking in its purely spiritual being—
Images from senses rendering, again, sensible treasures
Used to properly think thoughts from heaven seeing.

(*Only an embodied soul provides its full range of powers.*)

The united soul raises the body of a unique individual,
Eternity bound by God's spiritual gift; tho' once departed,

Our personality retained as a phantom residual
That resurrects the body from which it started.

What this glorified body will be like is only hinted at,
But, surely, it will be patterned after Jesus' body risen,
For in dying in Christ we will rise with him, a fact
We are assured of by the many scriptures given.

So the departed soul and glorified body resurrected
Are mysteries on which we should contemplate well;
A spiritual substance not quite angelic, but respected,
A body modeled on Christ's glorified one, as scriptures tell

Thus there is no dualism from God's creative act,
Only a unifying principle joined with the body to expand
Its powers to sense, think, and willfully act,
A phoenix arising at God's command.

Definitions

Being: that which exists, that which is. Beings can be material and mental, that is, "beings of reason" or a physical object in space and time. All beings derive from the first Being: God.

Dualism: the view that a person's mind and body are irreducibly different entities, or that physical and mental properties are of irreducibly different kinds. They are different substances. One is material and the other is immaterial in kind.

Form: that which provides a thing's uniqueness.

Higgs Field: the energy that pervades all of space that arose shortly after the Big Bang; could be thought of as "prime matter" from which everything arises. Einstein showed matter and energy were equivalent.

Self: the subjective manifestation of a human person that is a unity of body and soul, which is a spiritual entity. The first person "I" that we refer to when addressing ourselves. To a scientist, the self is a manifestation of brain processes; thus a subjective self is an illusion.

Soul: the primary principle of life, it is the form of the body and so is united to the body; it is part of our human nature. It is natural for the soul to be embodied, so that it can exercise its full range of powers; when separated from the body, it is incomplete. The mind is just one of the powers of the soul. The soul has activities that are not that of a corporeal organ—for example, the intellect isn't a capacity of the brain alone. The soul exhibits such powers as the intellect and the will. It is an immaterial substance that is spread throughout the body.

Subsistence: something that exists in its own right, not requiring another; that is, it exists independently by itself.

Substance: the "whatness" of something; that which primarily exists, exists per se and not in another. For instance, a cat has a substantive form; it exists by itself and each cat is unique.

Religion

A Catholic's Lament, Come Home!

God, the universe's Creator, His image dignifying men,
Deserves all glory and honor by us be faithfully paid.
Six days of work, but Sunday God rightfully demands
Our praise and service through Jesus, with the Spirit's aid.

Afraid of the personal sacrifices this love imposes,
Selfish wants and pleasures push such obligations away;
The wayward adore false gods, their souls exposed
To sin, and to Satan's siren song they give sway.

The Evil One: *"God will always love you no matter
how often you sin; and you surely won't die
if you eat of the world's forbidden fruits.
You have only this one life, take all it gives
with a haughty grin. You will be like gods,
it is only you that you must satisfy."*

So apathy, man's pride, and a waning lack of trust
Lead many to ignore proper worship of the Lord,
Pursuing worldly things and treating God unjustly,
Forsaking sacred relations and entry to heaven's door.

Catholics ignore the Mass' access to God's merciful love,
Its Great Thanksgiving honoring the Father, as we must;
Souls atrophy for lack of feeding here and from above,
As hope of becoming sons of God fades—turns to dust.

Jesus rising from the tomb renews faith's life promise,
So engage in what brings to Christian life its light:
Love of neighbor, forsaking of malice and resentment,
Humble service, and sacrificial worship, our call and delight.

Obeying the Father, Jesus freely offered himself in sacrifice,
Opening the gates to Paradise that Adam long ago lost;
Him, the model to imitate with our cross, His yoke is light;
Honor Him always in all things and ignore the cost.

From whence and why did Jesus come?

Jesus, God made flesh, the apex of salvation's history
Came from God's love of man that began with Abraham,
That righteous one of God, yet a profound mystery;
Father of nations and kings, chosen to save Everyman.

Israel, set aside (made holy), a nation of priests,
Typical of mankind that stumbles but keeps faith,
In Egypt grew to twelve tribes, forming the yeast
From which the "bread of life" arose, the key to heaven's gate.

In a burning bush, Moses encountered "I AM WHO AM,"
Who heard His people's cry and sent Moses to set them free.
Pharaoh felt God's power by plagues and Passover Lamb;
An enslaved people rescued by God's mighty deeds.

Moses, who spoke face to face with God, led the people out;
With manna and God's law the Israelites were fed.
A people of God tho' their faith was far from stout,
Stiff-necked, sin's slave, tribulations, by kings impiously led.

They ended with land and temple gone, yet His mercy felt,
Longing expectantly, the Messiah's time grown ripe:
David's kingdom renewed, land reclaimed and defended.
John baptizing, Christ's miracles, he's reliving Israel's life.

Jesus, the new Moses, calls for a new exodus from sin,
The Beatitudes expanding our vision and scope;
The son of David, who proclaims the "kingdom at hand" to draw
All men to him by grace, gave sacraments to help us cope.

He selflessly did his Father's bidding on the Cross to freely die.
The Lamb of God, blood of the New Covenant, men sanctified
As God's people—those humble in spirit and stripped of pride,
That show mercy—by Jesus' image, all Christians identified.

An hour a week we're asked to pray of our free choice,
Offering, with Jesus, our cares on the altar of sacrifice,
As the Spirit stays time and space, angelic choirs rejoice;
Bread and wine altered—the real presence of Jesus Christ.

But worldly lures and skeptical beliefs that rely on seeing
Dismiss the sacrifice that's being re-presented;
Scorning the Eucharist's essence effected by the Spirit,
Prayers become rote; sharing of one's time, resented.

But fallen away Catholics jeopardize their souls;
By blowing off the Lord's commands and church teaching
For a man-size god, they fail to renovate, aiming too low;
Unrepentant, they risk Gahanna for not upward reaching.

As selfish children, they claim their own authority
In deciding right and wrong, testing the Lord's reality.
"We don't need a cross; we now decide by a majority;
Your kingdom's passé in our personal freedom's centrality."

The mysteries of the Mass and the bread of life they forsake
For feelings, eloquent words, emotions, and fickle fellowship;
They forgo the "memorial sacrifice," yet subconsciously ache
For the "Bread of Life" and the liturgy's heavenly worship.

"Many are called but few are chosen; will there
be any faith when he returns? Not all who say Lord,
Lord will enter the kingdom, only those that do God's
will; The gate that leads to damnation is wide; They
are judged by their deeds."
(Matthew 22:14, Luke 18:8, Matthew 7:21, Matthew 7:13, Rev 20:12)

Christ's warnings fade, many Catholics flout the church
Built on Peter, the Spirit's gifts, and martyr's grief;
Spread by faith, zeal, and a Light heavenly perched,
Christ the Pascal Lamb, a church true to its apostolic belief.

Progressives in the church her authority reject,
Presume a few good deeds of charity and compassion
Will save them; Almighty God's majesty they neglect,
Eating their ruin, his Body and Blood, the Lord's Passion.

Beware, brothers and sisters, of the Lord's final Judgment
Unveiled in Revelation, a primer for this separating event;
Facing judgment for one's deeds; in agony, many will rue
Flaunting God's Will and Sunday's duty, in garments rent.

If Jesus is Lord of lords to be loved with abiding devotion,
The Mass should overflow with disciples full of zeal,
Catholic education sought by all, and joyful emotion,
As God claims Sunday and hungry hearts to fill.

Come Home! All are welcome!

The Shepherd's church has open arms for its lost sheep,
Calling all, the "Kingdom of God is at hand;"
Jesus asks, "Do you love me?" a reply he earnestly seeks,
Welcomes all home, tho' for many, it's unknown land.

Glorify Almighty God through the Spirit and the Son,
Edify your family on the Mass' great mysteries there,
Confess your sins, reconcile with God, from evil run,
With endurance, seek salvation, a golden crown to wear.

Dry Bones

Dreadful slumber, gloomy night, agitated, unaided,
Dreamt of desert, scattered dry bones, life here and there,
Ezekiel speaking of ages past as my fears abated,
Christians replaying Israel's folly, God dismissed with little care.

With vigor and conviction fading in Christians everywhere,
A dinky faith, it's no wonder dry bones are found.
The Master's words twisted to man's desires, no filial fear,
Toast-dry bones scattered, as worldly allures abound.

Christian spirit falls away, heaping more piles of bones,
Flesh bloated on worldly lures, yet spirit emaciated, nearly dead,
Salvific hope atrophies in the human heart, spirits moan:
Mighty struggles, the Evil One, lost souls, alarm and dread.

God sorrowful, yet always loving His Creation, expounds,
"Bones can come alive, people reconcile and win a crown!"
Ezekiel: "Your Spirit reclaims and the lost are found;
You enliven the spiritual dead whose bones are now aground."

"Dry bones, you're urged to heed the Lord's words again,
Reject worldly lures, repent of sins and guile, gain blessing,
Time is fleeting, harvesters gathering, let's anew begin;
Sing God's love song and in all nations spread His message."

I saw Christians who loved greatly earnestly praying aloud
For God's spirit's entry, that dry bones arise and come home;
Preaching, in love, God's salvific plan so lost were found,
And God, seeing true contrition, enlivens the dry bones.

The meeting of a risen Christian throng upon I gazed,
God's spirits invigorating those spiritually lost,
Bones knitted: sinews, flesh, covering skin—I was amazed!
Yet, some still lifeless, worldly grounded, shunned the Cross.

Despairing, I cried: "Almighty God show Your saving way!"
God relents, His spirit sent, bones spring to life bemused,
A vast army, forged in love, doing God's work without delay,
Heartfelt hope brimming, serving, yet many battered and bruised.

Awakening, hope in my heart once again leaps,
Accepting Christians' state of indifferent sophistry.
For in time, as I AM reigns, gathered will be His lost sheep
Through Christ's love, forming a gloriously woven tapestry.

Where Is He?
"Everyone is searching for you." (Mark 1:37)

Is this the plight of all today?
Those cast east of Eden in despair,
Searching for Him that loves,
Hearts restless among human affairs.

A world grown skeptical of God,
That claims dominion for man;
Fist held high in defiance,
"It is I," they shout, "who Am!"

Technology, pride, acclaim and fame
Makes gods of men, they confess;
Visibility is their reality test,
And God's control they detest.

Disillusionment and sickness set in
To depress and anger those obsessed
With things desired but lacking;
They secretly long for Love's caress,

Craving release from life's tribulations
That the world brings about,
Seeking spirituality's consolation
In counterfeit forms, lingering doubt.

Most are in life's Advent season,
Awaiting salvation promised to all;
But discerning not God's works,
They miss His whispered call.

"Everyone is searching for you."
They urgently proclaim aloud.
"Where is He in my need?"
Cry tormented souls, not proud.

Turn off your electronic gadgets,
Lift your heads from darkness' abode,
Shift your eyes to heaven's domain,
Make charity and respect your mode.

He's there when needed,
If you but search him out.
For Jesus came to save us from
The Evil One that roams about.

So answer Christ's clarion call,
Immerse yourself in words of life;
Humbly share, serving all,
And find peace in your daily strife.

Everyman's Call

One species living mutually,
Yet distinctions we erect,
Justifying acts of greed, envy,
To neighborly aid's call, no respect.

Balancing apathy and love
Regarding man's distress,
Helping ones deemed worthy,
Shunning those we detest.

Everyman's call for support
Reflects our Christian attitude:
Strangers helped for gain
Or aid given in gratitude.

All are in a "valley of tears"
Needing help, a loving touch;
Brother sheep, lost, scattered,
So don't shy away too much.

Heed Christ's call, aid Everyman,
For Jesus died for all.
Reject ingrained selfishness,
Answer Jesus' healing call.

Hear Christ's message; make
Love of neighbor your goal.
Reach out, reject exploitation,
Help make the needy whole.

Christ's call is expansive,
The world your concern.
God's people's suffering
Is ours to rightly discern.

"Good Samaritan" is our call:
A parable calming fears,
In pity, Samaritans nurse all,
Christ's intent superbly clear.

Be true lovers of people all,
Be not judged for selfish reasons,
Doomed for charity not shown,
Aid Everyman, in every season.

Fear of God

Gaining wisdom requires
A fear of God, I'm told.
He is an awesome God,
Too Glorious to behold.

Creator of the universe,
And earth her frame;
Awful in Majesty and Power,
Protective of His Good Name.

We owe Him reverence,
Praise, honor, glory, too;
Arousing in us to heed Him,
In all we say and do.

Indifference of Him abounds
Among the faithful throng;
Trivializing His Majesty,
Believing He will go along.

But He's jealous of His Name,
Which the past doesn't conceal,
When He raised in terrible wrath,
His Glory once again revealed.

So carrying a Christian name
Affords us God's assistance;
But it's conditioned on holiness,
Wills aligned, and persistence.

Fear of offending God
Or dishonoring His Holy Name
Should cause us to pause,
To live holy and without blame.

Thus in holiness and praise
Live our life secure,
Knowing that His mercy
To the faithful forever will endure.

Those Grown Weary

"Yet you did not call on me, O Jacob,
but you have been weary of me, O Israel.
But you burden me with your sins;
you have wearied me with your iniquities."
(*Yet He forgave those repentant.*) Isaiah 43: 21-22, 24b.

The West has grown weary
Of the Lord, the sacred remiss.
Worldly lures and sin abounding,
God's call and presence dismissed.

Indifference to God in daily life,
Bloated with confidence anew,
Many failed to call on Him
As man's worldly knowledge grew.

Yet our crimes and sins are manifest
For all to see in the nightly news,
As shame and boundaries are dismissed
And our debt grows, coming due.

Yet even after all we say and do
To offend God and our follow man,
He still loves us and will forgive
Those who repent, giving others a hand.

If not, the world will grow weary,
As our God does now with us,
And joy will drain away—
God's silence then, profoundly just.

If you want reprieve from the tedium
Of modern life, then prayerfully return
To Him whose message gives a plan
for life that men can joyfully learn.

Our country desperately needs
God's acumen, He to send;
Men flailing about to no avail,
Struggling, unwilling to amend.

Repair what greed and avariciousness
Has so profoundly affected;
A heart that's changed, love given,
And the Lord no longer neglected.

The Spirit's Role in Prudence

He sent the Counselor to make us wise,
So in acts of virtue we will find
The strength to do what is right,
And be found acceptable in God's sight.

It is through the grace of the Spirit's help
We learn of God's unending love,
That guides actions beyond our selfish self
And aligns our will with the Will above.

In a world where Satan holds sway,
We're to seek God's desires for humanity,
And we ask the Spirit's aid to keep evil away
From our thoughts and avert a soul's calamity.

For illumination, we seek through prayers
the Spirit's role in leading a virtuous life,
To inform our conscience and our hearts to care,
In difficult situations and when desire is ripe.

It is through the Dove's informing grace
That self-control and prudence win out,
And we can again look God in the face,
Doing what is right and just without a doubt.

So give thanks to the Father and Son
For sending the Advocate to our aid,
Gaining wisdom to know before an act is begun
What's right, leaving us no debt to pay.

The Other Brother

I heard that he was starving alone,
Feeding pigs, after squandering all,
In rags, a most dejected sight,
Agonizing over his fortune's fall.

The boy returning home exclaimed:
"Let me your servant and not a son be,
I'll work hard and I'll be no bother;
You'll treat me fairly, a servant not free."

Then the father's servant was asked,
"How was this forlorn boy handled?"
"My Master met him with open arms,
Clothed him, gave a ring and sandals.

"He celebrated, for him killed the fatted calf,
For a son was dead but now lived,
Heart overflowing with love, a kiss;
Boy's reply, 'Forgive me, Father, I have sinned.'"

"But what of the older brother's response?
How did he react to such display
Of the Father's welcoming arms,
And the affection shown that day?"

"Anger burst forth—he wouldn't go inside,
Unkindly listed his brother's many sins,
Complaining he'd been a faithful son
Receiving naught, so his brother wins."

A consoling father seeks understanding;
Those who serve are blessed by their call,
So jealousy and envy have no place
As God dispenses His saving grace to all.

"Son, you'll receive a full inheritance;
By endurance you've gained your gift,
Faithfully recognized and lovingly blessed,
Forbear a sinner's grace, be there no rift.

"Rejoice your brother has returned,
Be thankful he has come to the fold,
Don't enviously begrudge my generosity,
For a father's love, equally spent, enfolds.

"As a shepherd, if a sheep were gone,
You'd search high and low for him,
And finding that which was lost,
In jubilation would celebrate with your kin.

"As your mother on losing a silver piece
Would sweep the house up and down,
And on finding it, call friends to rejoice,
For the silver piece lost was found."

We must rejoice when sinners return—
God loves all men, those seeking Him most;
The heavens rejoice when men help those
Who call to God, and find Him in the Host.

The Number Three

Three, a central religious theme,
Made hallowed by the Trinity,
Patriarchs, magi, and days in the tomb
That launched believers into eternity.

God's nature is quite a surprise:
Father, Son, and Spirit that reveals
A family of persons and of love
That our body's temple conceals.

The Trinity is reflected ever anew
In the Christian family setting
Where husband and wife reside,
Love leading to children begetting.

The Patriarch three enlighten us,
Abraham, Isaac, and Jacob, too.
Faith, trust, and righteousness depict
What must be continuously renewed.

It was Jacob who fathered Israel,
His twelve sons' tribes fleeing
Egypt to claim its legacy,
With the Law and Moses leading.

Trials and tribulations their life,
As stubbornness and weak faith
Ended in exile in foreign lands,
Yet, in hope, the Messiah they await.

Time passes, a bright star appears
In the east, magi three alerted
To Judah's king-star rising,
They traveled west, disconcerted.

Looking for the king in Jerusalem,
Herod sends them on their way;
"Pay homage to the newborn King,
I seek news without delay."

The Star settled over Bethlehem,
The Holy Family quietly found,
Offered gold, frankincense, and myrrh,
Gentiles paid homage kneeling down.

The lad grows straight and tall,
At twelve in Jerusalem causes travail,
Missing three days, parents distressed,
In the temple, his Father's work to prevail.

His ministry is but three years long,
As the devil inspires the Pharisees' ire,
Innocent of sin, an unblemished Lamb,
His sacrifice praised by angelic choir.

The tomb can hold him but three days—
He descends to Sheol's dead; they're not to mourn,
For resurrection now theirs on Judgment Day;
Jesus rising on Sunday, humanity is reborn.

Given three theological virtues
To encourage mission work by all;
Faith, hope, and charity the call
To action that will prevent our fall.

Confirmation sends the Spirit's twelve fruits:
Love, joy, peace, patience, kindness, too,
With goodness, faithfulness, gentleness,
And self-control guiding us always anew.

We are given free choice to choose
Where we desire our eternity to spend,
Hell, heaven, with purgatory along the way;
Choose wisely, for there, life never ends.

So three is a vital number,
Telling of salvation's plan to take,
Symbolizing God and our central goal,
To know, love, and serve for eternity's sake.

Sam's Confirmation

First Audrey the Spirit she received,
Sarah and Tom following without fear,
Now Sam completes grandchildren four,
Confirming his Lordly trust, his duty clear.

Moses on Mount Sinai once climbed,
As the Spirit descended all around,
Receiving special graces and wisdom,
Faith filled, God's friend, tho' still aground.

And the Spirit descended at Jesus' baptism,
As God's voice announced to all:
"This is my beloved Son, in whom I am well pleased,"
So enters the Spirit today on the bishop's call.

As weak men frightfully huddled together
In the upper room locked and secured,
The house shook and filled with tongues of fire—
The Spirit making once timid men assured.

Likewise, we celebrate Sam's Pentecost today;
The Spirit's descent on all confirmed,
Strengthening each one in his faith:
To know, love, and serve God, again affirmed.

Accept the seven gifts of the Spirit today;
Those of wisdom, understanding, piety,
Fortitude, knowledge, counsel, and Godly fear,
Inform your faith while easing worldly anxiety.

From these gifts gain the matching fruits
Of love, joy, peace, patience, kindness, too,
With goodness, faithfulness, gentleness,
And self-control guiding you always anew.

Use these fruits to grow as a Christian man,
Forgetting not the God you affirm today.
Probe the depth of wisdom He has revealed,
Study always, serving God in all your ways.

You are called to be a soldier of the Lord,
Fighting a spiritual battle for your soul;
Know your weapons and the devil's snares,
Stand tall, courageous, and take actions bold.

As St. Paul tells us in an analogous way,
We're to strap on the Lord's armor together,
Remain steadfast in our faith and prayers,
And gain joy and happiness here and forever.

Avoid those who are lovers of themselves,
Who love money, are proud, arrogant, and profane,
Seeking only pleasure and power, forgetting God;
Search always for truth, faith and wisdom to gain.

So congratulations, my grandson Sam,
On this most auspicious occasion grand,
Let the Spirit fill you with grace and peace,
And may God keep you always safe, my man.

The Magnificent Seven Sacraments

Why and How?

Seven sacraments, life aids given by Christ
To His church, His earthly kingdom here,
Encompass all of life's diverse experiences;
Spiritual help to cope in our valley of tears.

Seven stands for the covenanting of parties;
Through Jesus' New Covenant graces expand
To cleanse and strengthen our souls and minds;
Material signs to unveil spiritual truths to man.

Sacramental signs use tangible symbols,
Divulging fantastic spiritual gifts hidden;
God's truths made visible through our senses,
Doing what they signify when rightly bidden.

An analogy to nature's energy enlightens;
It's stored in solid objects as energy congealed;
And try as we might through our senses,
We're blinded to its essence; itself concealed.
.
Similarly, the sacraments' spiritual realities
are hidden from our eyes and ability to feel,
Used are material signs and words to expose
A spiritual world which, tho' veiled, is yet equally real.

As Chesterton's paradox of humanness shows,
Sacraments are "certain and incredible," and bold;
For only the physical aspects are displayed,
Not the spiritual effects wrought upon our souls!

Incarnate Jesus is the quintessential sacrament:
God's Son made flesh to make known to us
The Father's personality for all to see and discern,
To guide use in words we've come to trust.

Jesus remains the greatest paradox to man:
Infinite yet finite, spirit yet flesh, God restricted;
A lion became a Lamb sacrificed for our salvation,
From death to life, an eternal contradiction.

He personified the sacraments in His life:
Baptized and confirmed in the Spirit and light,
Reconciler of God and man, forgiver of sins,
High priest, curing the sick, sinful lives put aright.

Like us in every way except for our sins,
Knowing our sinfulness and ways to amend,
Gave us sacraments that bring comfort and heal;
We'd be most wretched unless He, to us, attend.

Baptism

Those bound for the gates of heaven
Come through the baptismal font;
The first of the sacraments seven,
The freeing of sin is what it's all about.

Original sin and a willful tendency to disobey
Calls for a rebirth, a clean soul heavenly adorned;
In baptism, God's sanctifying love is made clear:
Sins washed away, souls reclaimed, and us reborn.

God's love was seen in parting the Red Sea,
Freeing His people from slavery and sin;
And Noah's ark kept safe a righteous remnant—
Washed free of sin, the world reborn, began again.

Christ's call is to repent for His kingdom's sake.
Baptized in the Jordan River, a dove appeared;
The Spirit blessed Him, our holy guide, and so
With Him to lead, we need not fear.

Jesus directs all be baptized to obtain salvation;
Initiated in the Father, Son, and the Holy Spirit,
And through cleansing waters and the Spirit's power,
Men die with Christ to rise again by His saving merit.

In an act of God's pure grace and abiding love,
Our souls are marked, we're made God's sons;
Sealed as Christians, our divine spark ignites and
Paradise is regained; through holiness the race is won.

Confirmation

Children of God learn, grow, and mature,
As love of their Savior grows in scope,
Always undertaking more mature things
For Him who died to find eternity's hope.

We study to be ready when our time arrives,
Confirmed in our faith by the Spirit's aid;
Armored with Christ, we live his mission out
With charity all our lives, our fears he allays.

At Pentecost, weak men in fear of reprisal hid,
Were amazed by the tongues of fire's descent,
Arose as lions for the faith, teaching unafraid.
Joyfully radiant, to the Spirit's lead they gave assent.

Confirmation is your own Pentecost event,
Receiving the Spirit's seal and oil of chrism,
Signifying adulthood in the church's body,
Authority and ownership of Christ's mission given.

From this point on expand your zeal,
Forgo laziness and spiritual sloth,
Seize on the hope of Christ's promise,
Seek what's valuable, a faith not lost!

Reconciliation

Jesus made His church and priests forever,
Men with power to act, a forgiving instrument.
So God and neighbor reconcile, mercy delivered,
Penitent moved by sorrow, forgoing all resentment.

In contrition, beg God to forgive transgressions,
For man has not the power to forgive his own sins;
Yet we can confess to a priest, *who can forgive*.
Accept absolution and make your needed amends.

Eucharist

At the Last Supper's gathering of apostles,
Jesus instituted a New Covenant, once, for all,
Bread and wine becoming His Body and Blood,
A cosmic mystery, raising man above the old law.

Not leaving us orphans in the here and now,
He, manna from heaven, true food that transcends
Space and time, feeds His flock until His Parousia;
To our Eucharistic prayer, we give the Great Amen.

Epiclesis and anamnesis prayers invoke the Spirit,
Memorializing Jesus' Passion, again re-presented,
Heavenly offering to the Father, perfectly acceptable,
Calls all to His Supper by His sacrifice's free consent.

In species of bread and wine transubstantiated,
We find His true Body, Blood, Soul, and Divinity;
Our Lord and Savior realized again for our good,
Heightening our holy desires, increasing our serenity.

No! We mustn't receive our Lord in mortal sin,
For then we eat our own destruction no less;
Reconcile with God and your brother and confess
Your sins, present your gifts, then Christ ingest.

Marriage

Marriage and children, the natural state for many,
Two people's covenantal relation accepted,
Freely entered into before God and man's witness,
God's Trinitarian nature on earth again reflected.

It is through the couple's words and conjugal pairing
That the spiritual benefits are received and expand;
Two selfish people become an ennobled *one*,
Blessings gained by entering God's co-creating plan.

Parents inform the domestic church in the family,
Rear and teach their children in faith and hope;
God's word is spread and the church replenished;
A people of God blessed with the faith to cope.

Anointing of the Sick

Man's lot, to earn his keep by his brow's sweat,
Resulted from original sin and Paradise lost,
Faced with a world of travails, aging, and sickness,
Yet comforted by the priest's anointing, at no cost.

Anointing of the Sick is open to the seriously ill who,
Through prayer and anointing oils applied,
Receive solace and hope for health's recovery;
With faith in God's power to heal, one can rely.

Holy Orders

Akin to marriage, the priest covenants himself,
His bride the church, his life the Lord's, no doubts;
Holy Orders initiate priest, deacons, and religious
Who serve God's people and spread the gospel about.

The priest, in "Persona Christi" at the Mass, calls
The Spirit, offerings changed into a heavenly meal,
With the people of God fed what angels desire;
A communion banquet, the Lord's presence real.

Know them well!

Seven magnificent sacraments remain essential
To our journey through life's ever twisting maze,
Constantly aiding our navigation back home
Through worldly lures, and the devil's beguiling ways.

Learn them well and apply them often
In your daily life and its perilous way;
Confess your sins, receive the Eucharist,
Study Scripture, evangelize, be saved.

Making Room

The priest asked:
Can you make room for him nailed to a tree,
Who died hideously to make us free?
The world rejected him at his birth,
No room in the inn or on the earth.
Do you reject him, too, having no space
In your heart and mind, no special place?
Why do you trust the world's wisdom
In place of God's love and forgiveness?

The devil's lures are manifold today,
But in the end, one is left a debt to pay.
For God is real and should be in our lives,
As our growing hurt makes us realize.
So stop, assess what's important now,
Carve room for him to enter—this allow.

Study, meditate, turn off electronic gear,
Let go of peer pressure and worldly fear.
Find God's love in Jesus' message,
Join in His love and gain His blessing.

God-Bearer

If a Christian, you're a God-bearer;
Baptism raised you up renewed,
Born again with spirit indwelling,
God's image now a part of you.

Baptism's token to heaven
Is stamped upon your soul;
You're part of his kingdom,
So God's growth allow, be bold.

The name "Christian" is awesome,
Sacredness and unity now yours;
Be worthy of it, don't profane;
Keep holy, reject your life before.

Value your body as God's temple,
For the Trinity it now contains;
Treat it with respect, allow no shame,
Keep it always spotless, don't defame.

As a God-bearer, become a love-giver, too,
Dispensing alms, charity, and prayers,
Witnessing Jesus to all you meet.
Be a drawing light, show you care.

Intellect, will, desires, and emotions
Conflict in the soul's judgment making;
So know God, form conscience aright,
Make holy choices by self-control taking.

God's image we carry in us,
And align our wills we must;
Christian called, we're God-bearers,
So with fidelity to God's Will adjust.

With clear conscience and heart,
In all actions display Christ.
Draw converts with compassion's light,
And bear His name with sheer delight.

Gloom and doom are not allowed.
For Christ brings us this hope that's sound:
Resurrected, glorified, renewed,
Eternal life—how can you possibly frown?

Part II

The People of God:
An Epic Journey

Introduction

God created Adam and Eve, and the people of God began the epic journey that is recited here. This epic poem is prophetic in that it recalls the events of salvation history. It employs Jeff Cavin's *Bible Timeline* as an outline. The story is cosmic in scope and vision. It is a great love story. And we must grasp the storyline if we are to understand who Jesus is and the role each of us plays. There is abiding love, strong emotion, heartache, drama, crisis, hope, longing, pathos, and great joy. In other words, it has all the elements that make a fascinating story, which is true, exciting, life giving, and interactive. We, too, are asked to participate in the story. It is a love song sung by God for His people—all those that strive for and reside in the kingdom of God; that is, those who accept Jesus as God's Son and do the will of the Father.

Man and woman were a kind of first fruit of God's Creation with their will and intellect aligned. But, after their fall from grace, Adam and Eve and their progeny were marked with a predisposition to sin. The will and intellect became misaligned and selfish desires became dominant. So very early in the story we find the human family choosing two different paths. One path leads to death as exemplified by Cain's seed, and the other path leads to eternal life as exemplified by Seth's seed (Adam and Eve's third son). These two paths are the counterpoints that are played out over and over throughout the history of man. Jesus described these different worldviews in an analogy to gates. The narrow gate, which is rough and few enter, leads to eternal life. The broad gate, which is wide and easy and many enter, leads to death. One path leads to angelic praises, while the other leads to the forlorn wails of the lost, due to the absence of love of God in the lives of those who chose it.

God is family, and Christian marriage fosters a family that reflects God's image on earth, yet, more, because we participate in the life of the Trinity. And God, in love with all Creation, forms a family relationship with mankind through His covenants. Throughout salvation history, God made covenants—Creation itself on day seven and then with Noah, Abraham, Moses, David, and finally, the New Covenant effected through the sacrifice of Jesus the Christ, the anointed one, the Messiah. The New Covenant represents a maturing of God's love for and trust in humanity, where He treats us as adults. It is through God's Kingdom, enlivened by Jesus at his death on the cross, that he expects His love to be expressed and spread around the globe and from pole to pole. The Kingdom is expressed in Jesus' church, which is the bearer of divine life to the world. Its people are chosen and consecrated to God for His purpose. "I (Jesus) consecrate myself, that they also may be consecrated in truth." (John 17:19)

To appreciate the story, we must absorb Old Testament types and truths that point to things and events in the New Testament. The Old Testament types become realized in Jesus, who recapitulates the story of God's people, Israel. So we must read the Old Testament in light of the New and the New Testament in light of the Old. Jesus made this abundantly clear in the gospels and on the road to Emmaus when discussing scriptures with the two disciples. Jesus and his church (in the context of salvation history, God's promises, and prophetic visions) proclaim the Good News of restoration and freedom. The history of God's people in the Old Testament is one of exile, bondage, and restoration as the people are released through God's intervention. The prophets pointed to a promised messiah, one who would free the people and renew the kingdom of David, which is now embodied in the Kingdom of God. This Kingdom is present both here on earth and in heaven, as are the people of God. The Kingdom, as promised, is made eternal through Jesus, who is the Good Shepherd of God's people. He knows his sheep and they know his voice and follow him by responding to his commands. So we are called to know, love, and serve God through Jesus' sacrifice and the working of the Holy Spirit.

Setting Context

Time Frames: Some important time periods and dates in Israel's history are as follows: <u>Abraham and Patriarchs</u> (2000 BC to 1700 BC), <u>Egypt and Exodus</u> (1700 BC to 1280 BC), <u>Desert Wandering</u> (1280 BC to 1240 BC), <u>Conquest and Judges</u> (1240 BC to 930 BC), <u>Royal Kingdom</u> (1050 BC to 930 BC), <u>Divided Kingdom</u> (930 BC to 722 BC), <u>Exile</u> (722 BC to 540 BC), <u>Return</u> (538 BC to 167 BC),

Maccabean Revolt (167 BC to 63 BC), Roman Occupation and Herod the Great (63 BC to 4 BC), Jesus' Birth (4 or 5 BC).

Power Structure: There was an ever-shifting power structure in the Middle East: The kingdom of Israel fell to the Assyrians in 722 BC, when the ten northern tribes were exiled and lost to history. Assyria and its capital, Nineveh, fell to the Babylonians in 612 BC. The kingdom of Judah fell to Babylon in 598 BC, and Jerusalem and Solomon's Temple were completely destroyed in 586 BC. The remaining Jews were then exiled. Babylon fell to Persia under King Cyrus in 539 BC, and some exiles from Babylon were allowed to return to Judah to rebuild the temple. This temple was rebuilt from 536 BC to 515 BC. As other exiles returned, the walls around Jerusalem were rebuilt by 445 BC.

Persia fell to Alexander the Great in 331 BC. After his death, Alexander's empire split apart in 323 BC. General Ptolemy ruled in Egypt and General Seleucid ruled in Syria. Syria defeated Egypt in 198 BC at Pamion and gained control of Palestine. The Seleucid king, Antiochus Epiphanes, ruled Palestine from 175 BC to 163 BC, and his rule led to the Maccabean revolt that started in 167 BC and lasted twenty-four years. Through this revolt, the Jews regained most of Judah. The reestablished Jewish homeland remained free until the Roman general, Pompey, captured Jerusalem in 63 BC and made Herod the Great Tetrarch.

The Major Prophets: The prophets arose during the time of the divided kingdom and the post-exile period. They called the people back to their history and covenant promises, foreseeing the demise of the kingdoms of Israel and Judah, if the people did not remember. They also foresaw the coming of the messiah. He would restore David's kingdom and free the people from foreign captivity. Much of Jesus' message concerned the exile and the freeing of Israel, not from Roman occupation but from the slavery of sin. Jesus came to set the captives free. The people were blind and in darkness, but now a new light shone in their midst. This searching and the need for the light of God to guide one's journey through life remain true for all generations. It is to be found in Jesus and his teachings. Christ continues to free Christians from sin in building the City of God, the New Jerusalem, here on earth. This means we're to put his words into action through love and self-sacrifice.

The following conveys, in poetic form, the journey of God's children through history to our present generation. Always and everywhere we are called to enter into the story for our own salvation and the salvation of the world. Bible quotes are from *The New American Bible*.

All God's Children

A story for the ages:
God's Kingdom is a mysterious thing, I think.
It's in us, as the spirit dwells, and we, as living stones,
Build up the church of God on earth—the link
To Christ, its head, and those that truly seek.
Christ's church of bishop, priest, and deacon,
Have served her faithfully throughout the ages,
Protecting faith's deposit without errors, a clear beacon;
A mother birthing Christians is adding story pages.
"How did this come about?" I wonder aloud one day,
This story of God's great love and His seeking us out?
It's about His children, with whom His graces stay,
"Narrow-gaters," Paradise regained, all that really counts.

Imagine:
What was it like on that first Creation morn,
When from nothingness a great light suddenly shone?
What did that illustrious light initially adorn?
God said: "Let there be light," and our world was born.

The Early World

I enter the story at its beginning long ago,
Before time ticked and anything was around.
God sang a love song, verses sweet and low;
On the universe, existence the Word bestowed.

"In the beginning was the Word." (John 1:1)

An awesome tune in God's mind arose;
It sprang forth from a single thought with power.
Notes added, the melody grew in His repose,
Erupting into a symphony of galaxies and stars.
It arose from pure love, nothing material then.
Suddenly, an awesome show, a "Big Bang"—it began,
Energy sprung from who knows where or when;
Six eventful days and Earth's full blown as men ascend.
Time appeared and space expanded then,

Atoms, stars, and galaxies materialized.
Earth, a habitat for man, just a void when
God's Spirit passes over and life begins.

The Milky Way, sun, moon, and Earth
Evolved per nature's rules that rightly amaze.
Flora and fauna, a planet's life given birth,
Who then sang a song of wondrous praise.
Oceans, continents, sun, moon, and sky,
Where birds fly and fishes play renewed,
And the earth splendidly carved, as eons pass by;
Creatures large and small refreshingly new.

*"God looked at everything he had made, and
He found it very good."* (Genesis 1:31)

Paradise sprung from a once uninhabitable setting,
Made up a "temple," God's work on display.
As Creation harmonized under God's vetting,
With man and God's wills in phase.
Day Seven God rests from His work as planned,
Covenanting with man a day in which to rest;
Elevating him above the beasts, his to command,
Decrees a worship day to protest the world's demands.
(*Mankind was called on Day Seven to accept
    God's authority and give Him praise in every land.*)
From dust, man took the form of flesh and bone,
Intellect, will, passions were then perfectly aligned.
In a garden paradise, he conversed with God alone,
Lacked for naught, a "namer" of things, which God condoned.
(*By naming things, man claimed authority over them alone.*)

*"The Lord…brought [animals] to the man to see
what he would name them…"* (Genesis 2:18)

Can you imagine what it was like then,
Seeing things new, a first for innocent eyes,
Fresh smells of garden delights awakening in him,
And tastes of strange foods everyday realized?

Happy, but incomplete, God puts things aright,
With Adam's rib raises up his missing mate,
Making a communion of spirits their delight,
Their garden life a paradise, fruitful and safe.
God invokes a covenant between them,
Exhorting them to multiply and fill the earth.
The most natural of urges a blessing then,
As sinless man first trod the virgin land.
God, Son, and their love, the Spirit,
Are reflected in the family that marriage manifests.
For two can bring forth a child to their merit,
Fruitful love giving life, meeting God's request.

Original sin:
Adam and Eve lived the perfect life of tranquil man,
When evil in their paradise came prowling about,
Tempting the woman, who doubted God's command,
And Adam, too, failed—ate of the tree forbidden.
Awareness of sin's effect came suddenly forth!
Nakedness clothed, they hid from the Lord.
God, knowing sin's impact, acts with no remorse:
Devil cursed, couple expelled, but left with hope.

"I will put enmity between you (the serpent)
  and the woman,
and between your offspring
  and hers;
he will strike at your head
  while you strike at his heal." (Genesis 3: 15)

"God did not make death, nor does he rejoice
in the destruction of the living. For he fashioned
all things that they might have being; and the
creatures of the world are wholesome...God
made man to be imperishable; the image of his
own nature he made him." (Wisdom 1:13-14)

The consequences to the human race were stark:
Innocence lost, concupiscence made present.

The tendency to sin now human nature marked
In man's elevated pride and desires unpleasant.
Sin spoils God's harmony decreed for all humanity.
Murder, strife, greed, and envy deny justice's demand.
Lust corrupts for the sake of wanton vanity,
And artificial barrenness flaunts God's command—
"Be fruitful and multiply," man and woman.
(*Sinners say in defiance of God: "I know what's*
*   right for me! I Am, they shout!" and elevate man.*)

Exiled:
By the sweat of their brow and labor pain,
Adam and Eve's days passed, as Cain and Abel came.
Herder and tiller, they raised animals and grain,
Praising God, offering products of land and rain.
(*In defying God, Adam and Eve lost their*
*   preternatural gifts, themselves to blame.*)
Yet, tragedy to Adam and Eve came around,
An envious Cain, chastised, a brother he kills.
Abel's blood cries out to God, tho' in the ground;
Cain sent east of Eden, his sinful seed abounds.
Seth, born of Eve, now passes on his seed,
Proliferates mankind, creating a holy line,
While Cain's seed leads to lands that bleed,
As sin infects them with selfishness and greed.

Two ways:
Here arises the two ways man may live his life:
One of holiness, the other of evil and eviction.
One, narrow and hard, leads to God's saving light,
The other, broad and easy, leads to man's perdition.
Prideful men try to make for themselves a name,
Stretched toward heaven, God's level to gain,
Build a Tower of Babel, seeking fleeting fame;
Language confused; wayfarers they remain.
God, observing His Creation's condition
Sees the evil designs of Cain's seed spreading
And debasing, a song sung in many renditions,
A dissident tune without love or appreciation.

*"By envy of the devil, death entered the
World, and they who are his possessions
experience it."* (Wisdom 2:24)

Life refreshed:
In sorrow, God seeks out a righteous man
To begin again and right man's evil ways.
It's Noah's family whom God chooses to expand,
And sends a chastising flood to rejuvenate the land:
'Twas a form of baptism, a cleansing of grievous sin.
By an ark Noah's life was saved from evil's design.
The world rid of sin rises refreshed again;
God's covenant renewed, the rainbow its sign.
Noah chose the narrow gate and found it hard,
Enduring jeers a hundred years to build his ark,
As mindless men held his family in no regard.
But, in trust, a just reward, he's to safely depart.
(*God asks for trust, patience, and our hearts.*)

The rains came, as God wept for His fallen Creation,
And for forty days and nights all was inundated.
A dove sent to find dry land, seeking an indication,
Plucked an olive branch, life renewed its implication!
With Noah's sons a rebirth of the world began.
From their loins nations sprang through time and space,
Passing the story to the Patriarchs and their clans,
As God's first born (Israel) feels God's saving grace.
(*The Savior had to come from a particular people;
    Israel was the nation ordained to show God's face.*)

Patriarchs

Abraham:
At Ur of the Chaldeans, by the Euphrates River,
The story resumes with Abraham, a righteous one,
Whose faith in God is secure as arrows in a quiver.
His clan travels to Canaan, a land to be delivered.
Being God's delight, he receives graces much,
As faith and trust gain a progeny when quite old.

Sarah laughed aloud, yet a child she was to clutch;
Isaac was blessed, while Ishmael fathered Islam, I'm told.

"God said to Abraham: 'As for the son of the slave
woman, I will make a great nation of him (Ishmael)
also, since he too is your offspring.'" (Genesis 21: 13)

Passing God's test in Moriah with Isaac, his beloved son,
Abraham's promised land, kingship, a worldwide blessing
To come from a future most mighty and holy one,
Who'll bring men an everlasting kingdom, possessing.

"I will make of you a great nation,
  and I will bless you;
I will make your name great,
  so that you will be a blessing.
…All the communities of the earth
  shall find blessing in you." (Genesis 12: 2-3)

It is Abraham's rectitude that's God's delight.
Father of nations, progeny multitudinous as stars,
That, by faith, he perceives in the bright daylight—
That which isn't seen but *is,* as faith requires.
Abraham's story has richness: He's promised land,
Rescues Lot, defeats four kings, receives Melchizedek's
Blessing of bread and wine, prefiguring God's plan—
true bread, Jesus' Body and Blood in believer's hands.

God's promises continue:
Isaac married his cousin, Rebekah, a fruitful one,
Birthing Esau and Jacob, contending twins.
Esau's birthright profanely sold, lentil soup the sum;
By a hairy ruse, a father's blessing Jacob won.
Animosity erupts; Jacob flees Esau's mounting rage,
Is himself tricked by Leban on his wedding day,
Seven years added for the one thought engaged.
His family grows, twelve sons begat along the way.
(*His sons came from free and slave, yet all were*
  heirs, a foreshadowing of the kingdom Jesus conveys.)
Jacob receives God's favor and a change of name,

He becomes "Israel," Abraham's covenant renewed.
He treks to Canaan, his ancestral land to claim,
As his family prospers in their expanding nomadic range.

Joseph, a favorite son, wore a many-colored coat;
Brothers' jealousy erupts, sold him to a passing caravan.
In Egypt, he's enslaved and jailed by his host—
Explaining Pharaoh's dreams he drew a royal post.
(*As Pharaoh's prime minister, he held the keys*
    of authority, as was God's plan to save Jacob's clan.)
Famine in Canaan brought the other brothers down
For Egypt's copious grain acquired by Joseph's wily ways;
Resulted in brothers contrite, a lost brother found,
And Jacob's reconciled family were soon Egypt bound.
A migration of Jacob's clan, some seventy strong,
Settled in Egypt four hundred years, learning a new song.
Grown rich, God's people were then done wrong:
Enslaved, to a tyrant's demand they now belong.

Egypt and Exodus

Slavery's pain:
Jacob's tribes a threat if Pharaoh is to thrive:
Thus Israel's firstborn, guiltless boys, are sacrificed.
Into the River Nile each to be plunged alive,
Yet an ark saves a son of Israel, death is denied.
A princess fair of Pharaoh's house, while bathing,
Espies the ark, Israel's savior, Moses, she claims.
Full grown, he explodes upon slavery gazing,
Kills an Egyptian, flees to the wilderness to remain.
In Midian, life starts anew watching sheep grazing;
He attained eighty years of age while growing desert wise.
An unconsumed "burning bush" he finds amazing—
Holy ground, I AM Who AM, as a call and fear collide.
(*Be ready for a call at any age—you'll have to decide!*)
God speaks! His people's cries to heaven rising
Calls for release, so Moses a trip will take.
Signs and wonder, forcefully God advising—
To Moses, "Tell Pharaoh, 'Let my people go!' for My sake."

Combat:
Pharaoh is obstinate: Moses' God he does not know!
Combat ensues with Egypt's nature gods on call.
They're embodied as plagues so Pharaoh will "know,"
God's awesome power trumps Egypt's gods, one and all.
The Nile River, denoting the fertile god Hapi,
Turns to blood before the Pharaoh's very eyes.
Undrinkable, parched thirst, all are unhappy;
Egypt's magic barren, no proper reply devised.
Similarly, nine plagues are in turn released,
As Egypt's gods become their personified source.
God displays His might, giving the people grief,
So Pharaoh "knows" Him and grant the slaves relief.
But Pharaoh's obstinacy lays on them burdens high.
He won't let them go afar to worship, as req'd,
Till a final plague brings death from the Egyptian sky,
Her firstborn to suffer as the angel of death passes by.

Passover:
The Lord's love of His "firstborn" is vividly shown!
Lamb's blood smeared, a sign upon Israelite's door,
As the "passover" of the angel of death skips His own;
The people prepare to flee, for they're now abhorred.
This merciful event is memorialized forever
In remembrance of God's love and freedom given.
It's God's awesome power that will save Jacob ever,
An event to tell all generations as they come together.

Passover rite prescribed:
A lamb selected on the tenth day of Nisan to behold,
Inspected for flaws until the fourteenth day unfolds,
Slaughtered, eaten as if at the first Passover, events retold
Of time long ago, re-presented as if in days of old.
(Jesus became the Passover Lamb to save mankind:
Palm Sunday occurred on the tenth of Nisan and He
was then inspected until the fourteenth day—the
flawless Lamb slaughtered at twilight on the Cross.)

People saved:
Lamb's blood saved Israel that terrible night,
As Egypt suffered what it had once inflicted
On God's newborn, justice again set aright.
Pharaoh freed them to worship God as they might.
Jacob's children arose. Leaving as soon as light,
A great migration to the Red Sea they march.
Pharaoh, raging at his loss, now spoils for a fight,
God intervenes, placing Pharaoh in a sea of plight.

"The Lord is a warrior,
  Lord is his name!
Pharaoh's chariots and army he hurled
    into the sea;
  the elite of his officers were
    submerged in the Red Sea.
The flood waters covered them,
    they sank into the depth like
      a stone." (Exodus 15:3-5)

Freedom obtained:
The Exodus began—Jacob's people going home.
Freed, they wander in the desert with Moses guiding,
Altered to trust, made battle ready as they roam.
At Mount Sinai a covenant ratified, the people abiding.
(*Israel is distinct, God is with them always; yet His*
  authority to set standard above man, rejected is.)

Desert Wandering

Nation forming:
They sang a new song as the wild desert they wandered
Learning to abhor Egypt's nature-gods. Inconceivable
for a generation to renew itself, is it any wonder
That trust faded in life's pains and freedom's lost luster?
Imbued with Egyptian beliefs after four hundred years,
They must be rid of them, if to God they acquiesce.
In the desert, their history is retold; all give an ear,
As elders are named and the people coalesce.

But they grumble at Moses in mistrust and fear,
Asking, "Why come to the desert to expire here?"
On seeing God's awesome power, sacrifice is now clear,
As their wandering is harder than it first appears.
(*They sang the blues in many variations, I hear.*)
God saved: thirst slaked, as Moses struck a rock,
And manna from heaven fed the unruly flock.
Yet they tired of the daily fare, grumbling at every spot.
So, with this stiff-necked people, God was peeved a lot.

Covenant that binds:
At Mount Sinai, God was gloriously to appear
In a cloud with lightning flashing all about.
People ran, earth shook, and all were beset with fear,
As Moses climbed into the cloud and completely disappeared.
(*God speaks from His glory cloud in salvation history
   to make His message clear.*)
Moses and God talked as two friends face to face.
He's given from God's finger Ten Commandments writ
To guide the behavior of the human race—
Honor God; treat each other with love and respect.

*"Hear, O Israel! The Lord is our God, the Lord alone!
You shall love the Lord, your God, with all your
heart, and with all your soul, and with all your strength."*
(Deuteronomy 6:4)

Moses codifies the law of the Lord that defined
His covenant: Land and prosperity his promise
If one obeys; many woes if disobedience He finds—
Destruction, dispersion, God's wrath of many kinds.

An unruly generation:
Moses' absence of forty days gave sway to latent activity—
Aaron coerced a golden calf to make,
Praised as the deity that led them from captivity,
As the people debauched themselves in ancient ways.
Coming down, Moses smashed the Ten Commandments there,
Golden calf ground to dust the people to ingest.

Levites arose as Moses raged, the people's sins now clear;
Family's priesthood lost; Levites new priests declared.
God's ire flairs, but Moses intercedes for their sins,
Saving them from death, but receiving God's chagrin.
Then God goes remote and Moses must pray within
the meeting tent, yet still speaks to God as a friend.
At Mt. Sinai, God's covenant was agreed to by all;
In blood sacrifice, the Israelites acquiesced,
Accepting its six hundred thirteen precepts (a holy life their call)
With its blessings and woes that lead to their downfall.
(*God's people were made holy, set apart, made a light*
   to draw all nations to God, if they're not to fall.)

"Taking the book of the covenant he (Moses)
 read it aloud to the people, who answered,
 'all that the Lord has said, we will heed
 and do.'" (Exodus 24:7)

Preparation:
An ark was precisely made, the law to hold;
Housed within God's prescribed tabernacle.
In the Holy of Holies, God's presence to behold,
And in front, a holy place, a court entirely enclosed.
Tribes forged into a military force, leaders elected
To occupy the land promised Jacob's descendants.
Seventy elders to judge Moses had selected,
As they wandered the desert, as God directed.
Stiffed-necked people were hard to change;
Disobedience and conflict regularly arising,
As pride riled against Moses' lawful reign.
People sentenced to wander forty years on the desert plain.
(*This rebellious generation would pass away,*
   their heritage not to gain.)
On Moab's Plains, a new generation assembles;
Moses tells of God's saving deeds and their obligations.
Battle tested, fighting force arrayed, enemy trembles
As Moses selects Joshua, the people's new foundation.
(*At this place, Moses predicts a prophet mightier than*
   he will arise to provide a new revelation.)

Conquest and Judges

Promised Land:
Joshua exhorts the people for a river crossing now—
The River Jordan parts, as the ark leads the way.
With Jericho's formidable walls, people ask, "How
Will such walls fall?" Trumpets blast them away.

Crossing the Jordan River at this point after
baptism, Jesus began his ministry:
"Repent, for the kingdom of heaven is
at hand." (Matthew 4:7)

Conquest varied, connoting lack of tribal trust,
Land partially conquered and settled as such.
Mixed marriages, idols abided, God's disgust,
As strife and woes stymied the tribal thrust.
The land was consigned by lot to each tribe.
Reuben, Simeon, Issachar, Zebulun, Dinah, Judah,
Gad, Asher, Dan, Naphtali, Benjamin in Canaan abide;
Joseph's heirs, Manasseh and Ephraim, to reside.
Time passes, catecheses abysmal, God ignored,
Strife with Canaanites and Philistines on the shore,
Uneasy peace—a condition commonly deplored—
People did what seemed right in their eyes as before.
(*Dissident notes were heard through the land once more.*)

Judges and Kingdom:
Tho' tribes unfaithful, God aids in desperate ages,
Elevating judges to save the people for awhile:
Othniel, Deborah, Gideon, Samson, not all sages.
Yet God's mercy eases their misery, say the Bible pages.
The last judge, Samuel, takes Israel into a new age.
Beloved of God, a mighty prophet and holy man,
Accedes to the call for a king, then all the rage
In other lands, anoints Saul, as the kingdom age began.
They reject God as king for one adorned with a ring,
As God condescends: Anoint earthly ones for now,
Until Jesus makes God, evermore, King of kings
In his Heavenly Kingdom, a Messianic age to bring.

Royal Kingdom

Tribes unite, Saul pacifies the nations around,
But his pride leads to a ruinous fall at a later date.
David "rocks," brings Goliath down, his fame abounds,
As Saul's lost accolades turn envy into hate.

As the women sang: "Saul has slain his thousands,
and David his ten thousands." (1 Samuel 18:7)

Wilderness:
A game of hide and go seek in the desert ensues,
With Jonathan aiding David, a friend he loves.
He stays Saul's design; David pitilessly pursued,
Yet his love twice spares God's anointed one.
Philistine's animus toward Israel arises again;
Samuel's late, Saul asks an oracle, who wins?
He thus loses God's favor, as a decisive battle begins;
All's lost—Saul and Jonathan dead, David ascends.

Davidic Kingdom:
Samuel anointed David based on the tribes' consent;
A new king proclaimed, God's chosen dignified.
He dispatches Israel's enemies, a unifying event;
Obtains peace, with Jerusalem now fortified.
(*At thirty, David becomes king and at thirty, Jesus starts*
   his ministry where he will be glorified.)
King David given a covenant of God's devising:
A kingdom lasting ever, sired from Jesse's root,
Given in perpetuity to Jesus on his death rising:
An awesome event consummating God's plan for man.
Ecstatically, to Jerusalem David brings the ark down,
Dancing in utter delight before the procession bold,
Praising God's law and His eternal mercy shown.
David offers sacrifices like the priest-king of old.
He badly sins with Bathsheba, the object of his desire;
In deep sorrow, sin confesses, is penitent and contrite.
Forgiven, tho' son of sin lost, another son he sires—
Solomon—to occupy David's throne when he expires.

Disorder reigns in David's house as sons rebel;
Death and tragedy stalk David's declining years.
In tears and agony is the story he's left to tell;
Dying, Solomon the new king the tribes loyally hail.

A sad end:
Solomon asks for wisdom to mark his reign;
Wise for a while he expands David's range.
A marvelous temple erects, world fame to gain,
As Israel's light shines forth, becoming its enemy's bane.
Foreign alliances and seven hundred wives defame God's law,
With mixed marriages ensnaring him in idol worship.
God denied, wisdom gone, he cruelly taxes subjects all,
Planting seeds of disunity, a kingdom set to fall.
His son, Rehoboam, haughty, cruel—ambitious, too—
Ignores sage advice and by a younger group is badly led.
Compromise flouted, northern tribes he cannot woo;
Ten tribes secede, leaving him alone to sing the blues.

Divided Kingdom and Prophets

Growing malice:
The northern kingdom, Israel, its name retained,
Crafted golden calves, igniting latent flames.
Samaria the capital the people religiously retrained
To avoid seeking Solomon's Temple and its fame.
In the south, the kingdom known as Judah resides.
Jerusalem its capital, the temple avowing God's law.
The Covenant, while maligned, isn't set entirely aside,
But David's house struggles with idols before its fall.
The north and south endure uneasy peace and strife,
Neither gains nor ameliorates each other's gripes;
Ominous foreign threats arise and danger grows ripe;
Nine dynasties, house killing house, a dirge is piped.

Northern demise:
The north is afflicted by numerous abominations,
Sacred poles and gods worshiped in high places.
Baal, the one adored, adopted from other nations;

Babies consumed by fire, God's wrath awakens.
God raises up a mighty prophet, Elijah by name,
Giving him a full portion of power and sight
To fight the evil in Israel, to its shame,
Calling people to repent and to put things aright.
But with King Ahab and Jezebel, evil lurks
As Elijah rails against their Baal devotion;
Their god belittled, priests slain, Jezebel berserk,
Hunts the one who did God's whispered work.
Elisha follows Elijah endowed with a double portion;
He cures the sick and raises the dead to life,
Foreshadowing the power and devotion
To God shown by Christ when his time was ripe.
Assyria's ambition sees Israel as a dessert to be,
As harlotry again abounds in David's land.
Jonah goes to Assyria to save; ravaged cities sees he,
If the Israelites fail to repent as God commands.
Israel by Assyria is defeated, northern tribes exiled,
As foreigners claim the Promised Land,
Intermarrying with the remnant of people lawfully defiled,
Mixing religions and foreign gods all the while.

Southern demise:
The south vacillates between good and evil kings,
As foreign gods and poles on high pollute the land.
Prophets—many—forewarn of coming dark things:
Babylon to destroy the temple, expelling Judah's clan.
A great catastrophe engulfs all of Judah strongly—
Starvation, cannibalism, and slaughter great ensue.
Defilement its fate, as the princes treat God wrongly;
People exiled to Babylon, Canaan void of its elitist Jews.
(*Judah's exile from God's presence: a physical reality
    reflecting the spiritual reality of sins pursued.*)

Prophets forewarn:
Derided were the prophets in the north and south
That spoke of trials, destruction, and debacles to come
Unless trust and praise formed again in their mouths.
Alas, prophetic oracles fulfilled, as many woes go south.

Each prophet called the princes and kings back
To the law and proper temple liturgical rites,
Citing abuses of the lowly, a deplorable fact,
And babies sacrificed to foreign gods, a horrific act!
Foolishly, princes scorn the "Jubilee's" slave release,
As they are briefly freed, mocking the law.
Nation poorly led, it becomes an Assyrian feast;
God's ire is up and the nation-Israel travels east.

Isaiah laments of Israel's impending doom,
Gives hope David's kingdom to resume;
A suffering servant to dispel oppressive gloom,
And mankind to rejoice in the Kingdom's Good News.
The prophets point to the Messiah's coming,
David's kingdom rising from Jesse's branch.
Jeremiah sees Judah thriving, land humming;
The Shepherd's sheep leaping joyfully in a dance.

Exile and Prophets

Woes north and south:
Two centuries before Judah's fall in the south,
Assyria despoiled and expelled the northern tribes.
Israelites dispersed, defiled by nations round about;
Religious practices mixed, with God's law pitched out.
Rachel wept at Naphtali, as Assyria dispersed
Ten tribes to the nations, forever lost, never found.
A judgment on abominations they'd failed to reverse,
Yet hope of return abounds; prophets see a turnabout.

Jerusalem barren, the implausible occurs somehow,
The Promised Land despoiled, devastation all around.
Like docile sheep Judah's elite led to new pastures now,
A people divested, distraught, as total dismay wins out.
The joyful tune of David's day now sung as a dirge;
Cities devoid of their elite, only the poor remain.
Rachel weeps at Ramah, her children to emerge
Dismayed in a foreign land, as despair stakes its claim.

Exile and hope:
And so by the river Chebar, Ezekiel gives exiles hope
Of God's mercy and David's kingdom restored.
People called to holiness and duty aren't to mope,
But be their brother's keeper, helping each other cope.
The prophet Ezekiel tells of God's displeasure,
His shepherds ill-treated His sheep.
God, as Shepherd, allots justice in full measure;
He'll give Israel back its land to keep,
Temple to be rebuilt so God can reside there again,
His glory to settle over the Temple Mount,
A new covenant inscribed on hearts within,
And from the Temple living waters to flow out.
(*Jesus, the new temple, is the living water's font.*)

In Babylon, Daniel dreamt of four devouring beasts,
Eastern powers who were bettered by one
"Like the Son of Man;" his authority, once increased,
Gives Israel a dominion that will never again cease.
Daniel foresees a day when Israel sparkles like new,
As the Son of Man gathers the clans from afar.
Gabriel declared a period of four hundred ninety years to renew—
Jeremiah's seventy years to begin the final accrual due.
(*In four hundred ninety years, Jesus' ministry will Israel renew.*)

Return and Prophets

Return begins:
Jeremiah envisions Israel's return, a paltry few;
Babylon falling, King Cyrus the tool God would use.
Judah's remnant chartered, God's temple to renew;
Zerubbabel, their shepherd, built as the trickle grew.
(*He is in David's line that leads to Christ, who is
    everlasting life's clue.*)
Impeded by Samaria, which grew afraid
Of a fortified city, grumbles and interferes.
Vexed, Nehemiah comes to the people's aid;
Walls and temple erected, the law again revered.
Ezra, the scribe, re-catechizes, law reads aloud;

People sob at their loss, but now would reclaim.
The unevenly yoked, divorced, idols divested if found;
Jews set apart, Ezekiel's temple liturgy proclaimed.
(*Holiness is Gentile separation and living without blame.*)
The new temple symbolized God back in the land,
A time of restoring Judah's faith and surrounds,
As temple worship unifies the people, a growing band;
The idea arises that the messiah's advent is at hand.

But ages pass, shifting powers the reality of the land,
As Greek city-states emerge as a potent threat.
Persia struggles to conquer Greece's mighty clans,
Meets victories and defeats as hostility expands.
From Macedonia comes a young and ferocious king,
Alexander by name and a warrior of eternal fame;
Destroying the Persian hoard, his praises we still sing,
A juggernaut sweeping east, Hellenizing as it came.
At Alexander's death, quarreling generals split apart.
Rivals, Egypt and Syria, connive and contend;
Ubiquitous conflicts erupt from its cleaved start,
And the Seleucid, Epiphanes, stokes tensions within.

Maccabean Revolt and Rome

Aberrant ideas fill Judah and many Jews relent,
As time passes and Ezra's religious influence wanes.
Greek culture bedazzles, yet it's hated by Jews who resent
Its debasing effects, raising resistance, but in vain.
Aided by Jews who want only accommodation,
Epiphanes profanes—all to partake of Gentile worship.
His ploy: to destroy Judaism by active Hellenization,
As threats and sacrilege cause religious zeal to slip.
(*The people went along to get along, their trials to skip.*)
All loyal Jews are to eat of sacrificial swine.
The temple's profaned by Gentile worship there,
And envoys build, everywhere, new shrines,
As people are forced to eat the pig prepared.

Uprising:
In Modein, the envoy offering sacrifice one day
Met the Maccabeus' clan, who refused to forsake
Their Lord; fury aroused, they devour with dismay,
Fleeing, rebellious men rally for liberty's sake.
Open rebellion quickly turns to armed resistance,
Where, tho' outnumbered, victories are theirs:
Gained through faithfulness and sustained persistence,
Trusting in the Lord as Abraham's rightful heirs.
Mighty battles follow until Jerusalem is won,
Enemies defeated and the temple again sanctified.
Sanctuary purified, altar anointed, and worship begun;
Citadel stormed, Judah freed, enemy on the run.
(*Hanukkah celebrates these events under today's sun.*)
From this time, until the Romans invade to stay,
Judah freely worships God, but mortal threats remain
From neighbors and those vexed, who would betray.
John Maccabeus elevated high priest, the one now to obey.

Enslavement and longing:
Threats and pressure from enemies deployed all about
Forces ill-advised alliance in hope of saving aid.
Gives Rome a ploy to destroy, Judah's freedom loses out;
Tho' free to worship, a tyrant's yoke the awful price paid.
(*Human yokes chafe, Jesus' yokes fit through grace's aid.*)
Subjugating their spirit was hard to do,
Knowing they were the beloved of the Lord.
Jews restless under Caesar, who sullied anew—
Roman cohorts given land promised to the Jews.
Hope for the messiah and David's kingdom restored
Is rife among the people, as was foreseen.
Hope runs high, Jews long for glory once more
As daggers pierce hearts dejected and forlorn.

*"Oh, that out of Zion might come the
     deliverance of Israel!
That Jacob may rejoice and Israel be glad
     when God restores the people!
(Psalms 53:7)"*

Messianic Fulfillment

On hearing the people's cries of a captivity they resent,
God sends a Savior, born to die by his own consent.
As they'd killed His messengers, God's Son was sent
To release Israel—the Incarnate One, God is present
(Emmanuel).

"For God so loved the world
that he gave his only Son,
that everyone who believes in him might
*   not perish*
but might have eternal life." (John 3:16)

Mary and Joseph live in the land called Galilee,
Heritage land of ancient Israel in the north.
Mary, blessed with child, God's Son to be,
With Joseph, treks to Bethlehem as Caesar decreed.
God's glory overshadows Mary, as it did over the
Meeting tent and Holy of Holies in the temple. Mary,
The new ark of the covenant, conceives the Word, he
Who becomes the Savior of the world she is to carry.

"Rejoice, O highly favored daughter! The Lord is with
you. Blessed are you among women…Do not fear, Mary,
you have found favor with God. You shall conceive and
bear a son and name him Jesus." (Luke 1:28-31)

The Messiah is born:
A star appears in the eastern sky, read by magi three,
Who then pursue Judah's star rising in the west.
They seek the King, the Savior who was foreseen:
In Bethlehem, Gentiles kneeling, evoke a salvation scene.
He is born in the "city of bread," as foretold,
The "bread of life" angels hail, shepherds' delight.
Gifts of gold, frankincense, and myrrh given, I'm told,
Fit for the Priest-King, a fallen world to set aright.
Thus the Incarnate God is born in a stable poor,
As the world has no room for the Savior at its door.

The Child radiates love on all who come to adore;
At twelve, he amazes the temple's elitist core.
Like Pharaoh, Herod killed guiltless boys, a threat to him,
And Joseph fled to Egypt, his family there to save.
Thus Jesus comes out of Egypt to free Israel again
As of old, a new exodus, the world his to amend.
He's an obedient child in Nazareth his home;
A laborer of no apparent education or worth.
Yet he shines with wisdom unsurpassed, his alone,
Doing miracles, singing Isaiah's suffering servant song.

The prophet Micah declared Elijah would return
to proclaim the Messiah had come to restore
David's kingdom, gathering lost sheep that yearn
To reclaim their land and to restock Abraham's core.
John the Baptist (Elijah) seen in the desert crying:
"Prepare the way of the Lord, make straight his path.
Repent, the Messiah's here, the old way is dying."
At Jesus' baptism, a dove signals hope's come at last.
(*A dove gave Noah an olive leaf, a world renewed;*
   this dove reveals the End of the Age by contrast.)
Jesus, the "new Israel," is tempted in his desert flight;
Unlike Abraham's children of old, he passes his test,
And we hear God assert: "He's My Delight,"
Destined to save the world from its awful plight.

"Not on bread alone is man to live
but on every utterance that comes
   from the mouth of God…
You shall not put the Lord your God
   to the test…
You shall do homage to the Lord
   your God;
him alone shall you adore." (Matthew 4:4-10)

The kingdom at hand:
"Repent, for the Kingdom of God is at hand,"
Is the Good News that Jesus publicly proclaims.
As rumors of his miracles circulate in the land

Enticing large crowds, his cures in high demand.
(*The crowd is excited, crying: "Is this the man?"*)
He's the new Moses, giving a new law to guide.
Tho' God's first law still applies, Jesus raises the bar
By his Sermon on the Mount: love to abide
In humble hearts and where thirst for justice resides.
In the Beatitudes we're called to this fact ingrained:
Blessings come not in selfishness or worldly fame,
But in giving oneself in mercy, a new life to obtain
In a Kingdom of pure hearts, as Jesus proclaims.
On a mount Jesus gave a sermon divine,
With the people reclining humbly about.
Through his words Jesus' image is enshrined,
The Beatitudes flashing new visions in every mind.
He commands us to help one another in love,
Actively calling us to aid others and be changed.
We gain eternal life by serving, acting as a dove
To all mankind, imitating our Father above.
He says not to retaliate but to love thine enemy,
As anger leads to revenge among men,
Causing murder, animosity, and infamy;
We must forgive, as only love amends.
Wills aligned, from the Evil One he'll defend.

"Seek first his kingship over you,
his way of holiness, and all these
things will be given to you besides."
(Matthew 7:33)

Jesus came to restore David's kingdom of old,
And to reunite the twelve tribes, if truth be told.
He dons Israel's iniquities, his life he sold,
Redeeming a world grown devilish and cold.
(*Jesus accepted the curses of Adam and Israel; he*
   ransomed men so Paradise is found, so be bold!)
Jesus' rule: act from mercy, not to gain praise,
Rewards are in heaven or earthly ones alone.
Choose by your deeds—the good or evil you raise.
Go for piety, skip fame, if it's Heaven you crave!

(Few believe God will judge them for what they do,
   saying: "He'd not cast us into hell, only the depraved.")

Listen to him!
Jesus teaches of the Father and heavenly desire,
And how to forgo judgment by loving thy neighbor.
As "fruit inspectors," we're to reject all that sire
Evil intentions—flee from them, escape Gahanna's fire.
Faith filled, we're sent to heal the culture,
Donning God's Armor so it won't fatally sicken us,
Mingling with fellow sinners to give them a future
By proclaiming the gospel left in our trust.
(Jesus spoke in parables to a corrupt generation,
   describing his Kingdom for people like us.)
Jesus' kingdom parables allude to many things:
It's like leaven, a mustard seed, infested with weeds.
It's in us, the world, Heaven, in Christ our King,
And in his church and the Eucharist it brings.

Life's bread:
Jesus, manna from heaven, set at God's right hand,
Feeds us his words and sacramental Body and Blood
That's foreseen in His feeding of thousands in Israel land,
Displaying his power as he calls on God above.
A large crowd has no food their hunger to slake, so
Jesus multiplies loaves and fishes for them to intake.
They're fed so not to faint as homeward they make.
Of Jesus, the bread of life, we, too, can partake.
(His Body and Blood feed us on our journey so we
   won't perish on the way we take.)

"Let me solemnly assure you
if you do not eat the flesh of the Son
   of Man
and drink his blood,
you have no life in you…
He who feeds on my flesh
and drinks my blood
has life eternal,

*and I will raise him up on the last
Day."* (John 6:53-54)

Jesus, the new temple, is also its sacrificial meal,
Who raised the temple up in three days, renewed.
He's a conundrum the world has trouble accepting still,
As faith to see the truth fades with our spiritual zeal.
(*Lord take away my unbelief, help me believe you're real!*)
But, before Jesus to Jerusalem goes to meet his fate,
He appoints a prime minister until he comes in glory,
And Peter confesses Jesus the Christ, time grows late,
As the Lord cedes Peter the Keys, his to delegate.

*"You (Peter) are 'Rock' and on this rock I will build
My church...I will entrust to you the keys of the
Kingdom of heaven."* (Matthew 16: 18-19)

His Glory shown:
Jesus goes to the mountains, his divinity to show,
Where, transfigured, Jesus glows as white as snow,
Converses with Moses and Elijah about his departure.
Peter, James, and John, wishing them to remain below,
Would erect booths; his glory they'd recall in the future.

(*The Transfiguration experience lets the apostles
profess that Jesus died of his own volition, while the
booths relate back to Israel's commemorating their
first departure from bondage in Egypt.*)

His hour has come:
On an ass, he enters Jerusalem, as Solomon before,
To the cheers of people strewing palms all around.
The Lamb without blemish, hosannas galore;
Betrayed by fickle men, as evil owns this ground!
Jesus speaks boldly, as only the Son of God can,
Attaining for himself the condemnation of man.
A challenge put that the Pharisees can't let stand,
As they hatch a plot to kill him using Roman hands.
The apostles, elevated to priests to forgive man's sins,

Will preach the gospel from Jerusalem to land's end.
New Covenant given in Jesus' blood now begins
With the Last Supper; later he's betrayed by a friend.
At the Passover meal with the Apostles (called ones),
He changes bread and wine into his Body and Blood,
The Eucharist to feed his sheep for all ages to come.
He teaches them to serve his church that's now begun.

*"Took bread, and after he had given thanks broke it
and said, 'This is my body, which is for you.
Do this in remembrance of me'... He took the cup,
saying, 'This cup is the new covenant in my blood.
Do this, whenever you drink it, in remembrance
of me.'"* (1 Corinthians 11:23-25)

In a garden, Jesus is tempted by evil's stain;
But, unlike the old, the new Adam is justified,
Gaining man's salvation, while in agony sustains
His Father's will: tried, scourged, and crucified.
(*This act replays Adam and Eve's temptation in the
Garden where they failed; righteousness Jesus regains.*)
Arrested by the temple guard upon Judas' kiss
And brought to the Sanhedrin, as Peter enters its gate,
Denying him thrice as the cock crows, things amiss.
Jesus enters the devil's den, as Satan's hour grows late.
Before Caiaphas, the high priest, he's falsely accused,
Now speaks openly: "I *am the Son of God to reign!*"
Pilate scourges, cries to crucify him not refused,
At Golgotha, nailed to a tree, little life remains.
(*The Tree of the Cross is the Tree of Life for those that
   accept Jesus as Savior and make his work their aim.*)
"Father, forgive them, they do not know what they do;
Woman, this is your son; I thirst; it is done."
Sky darkens, earth quakes, temple's curtain torn in two—
"Truly this was the Son of God, the King of the Jews."

The Resurrection:
Like Jonah in the whale, Jesus entombed three days,
Shroud draped in a new sepulcher, guarded.

Descending, holy ones fetched to Heaven to stay;
Rising, gives hope we'd rise too, with some delay,
Our soul embodied and glorified as the scriptures say.

Alleluia, he's risen:
He is seen by Mary Magdalene, who to the others fled,
And deciphers the scriptures on the road to Emmaus,
Where two men know him in the breaking of the bread,
And in the upper room, his peace to the disciples he bade.
We're told the story of doubting Thomas, who had to see;
But truth be known, we, too, ask for a sign so as to believe.
Jesus gives only the sign of Jonah and the Spirit to a degree,
So, in faith, accept him as Lord and from your sins be set free.
Fishers-of-men are to extend the kingdom everywhere,
By witnessing through their love—a light to call men
To his church, baptizing in water and Spirit there,
And offering a perfect sacrifice, saying, Amen! Amen!
(*The church is the Kingdom's earthly presence where*
    Jesus is head, high priest, and perfect sacrifice for men.)

The Church

"We are children of God. But if we are children,
we are heirs as well…if only we suffer with him
so as to be glorified with him." (Romans 8:16)

The Kingdom given into the Apostles' hands in trust;
Forty days, Jesus tells them how scriptures are fulfilled.
And gives the Great Commission: disciples must
Baptize in the Trinity, gospel spreading their thrust.
(*We are to attend the sacrifice and sacrifice ourselves*
    to extend God's love to Everyman, his words not to hush.)

"If you find that the world hates you, know it has hated
me before you. If you belonged to the world, it would
love you as its own; the reason it hates you is that
you do not belong to the world." (John 15:18-19)

Pentecost:
Before his ascension to sit at God's right,
Apostles granted power to forgive sins here,
Awaiting the Paraclete to bring all truths to light.
Later, they preach the Word while calming fears.
At Pentecost, weak men in fear of reprisal hid,
Are amazed by the tongues of fire's descent,
Arise as lions for their faith, now teaching unafraid,
Joyfully radiant, to the Spirit's lead give assent.
At the first Pentecost, Moses received the law
For God's people; at the second Pentecost, the
Church, Christ's Body, a new law of love they saw
That invited all to participate, so as not again to fall.
Peter and the apostles astonish the crowd there.
Speaking, they are heard in each man's native tongue
Attesting to God's Son made Incarnate here
To redeem; reborn as men united, freedom won.
(*The Tower of Babel was now reversed, as men could
    understand and reunite by accepting God's Son.*)
Crowds of believers coalesce around Peter;
The "way" spreads, as all gather in communion,
Hearing the word and breaking bread, they enter
Into the kingdom to build up Christ's dominion.

*"Behold, now is the acceptable time; behold, now is
the day of salvation."* (2 Corinthians 6:2)

*"You are a chosen race, a royal priesthood, a holy
nation, God's own people…Once you were no
people, but now you are God's people."* (1 Peter 2:9)

Missionary zeal:
Jewish leaders upset by the rapid spread of this sect
That draws people from their power, casting doubt
Of their crucifying Him, whose startling effects
Shine in love and cures that all, in awe, talk about.
Audaciously, the Apostles speaking of Jesus' rising
Riles Paul, who elicits the stoning of Stephen,
Whose martyr's blood seeds growth, spreading

The faith to Rome, a Spirit-guided, fruitful season.
On Damascus' way, Paul finds the Lord quite real:
A flash, "Saul, Saul, why do you persecute me?"
An encounter that fires Saul's missionary zeal
To convert Gentile sons, the faith to reveal.
Paul proclaims that Jesus is doing a new thing;
The people are no longer under the old law,
But are freed by Christ's sacrifice; everything
Is new for those who repent and receive the call.
The church's foundation, apostolic faith ratified;
Tho' widely scattered, it's one body in Christ,
With one liturgy—word and Eucharist unified.
On Sunday faithful are called, fed, and energized.
The church is where truth is quantified.

*"You will know what kind of conduct befits a
member of the household of God, the church
of the living God, the Pillar and Bulwark of
Truth." (1 Timothy 3:16)*

Jesus names the apostles as bishops to lead
His flock; small at first, growth leads to priests,
With deacons aiding as expansion decrees;
The church rises on the Spirit's energizing yeast.
Peter and Paul in Rome witnessing to Jesus,
The one crucified, who calls sinners to his side;
They die as Nero's martyrs, called to give, like us,
A measure of sacrifice and in faith to always abide.
From martyr's blood sprung a church militant,
That through the ages grows in size and global wide.
Under Peter's Chair auspices, it is resilient,
A reliable repository of faith, none set aside.
(*The church calls us to image Jesus, reaching
    skyward, not dragging God down to man's size*)
His church honors the Father, not fickle man,
Imaging Jesus so God's Will will be done on earth.
It's built of living stones, those helping hands
That spread the gospel of love, as he commands.
The church gives us manna, Jesus' real presence,

The Eucharist: a Holy Banquet to feed his sheep;
Life's bread with power to renovate, Spirit sent
Through an heavenly worship she faithfully keeps.

The Story Goes On:
If you're baptized, you're part of this story,
So join in faithfully and with martyr's zeal.
Bestow love of neighbor for the glory
Of the Father and make your mercy real.
(*Jesus came, and so we're called to reconcile man*
    with God by the mercy shown and faith fulfilled.)
The song started by God's internal harmony
Has grown in size and musical diversity.
Each Christian adds his note in conformity
To Jesus' call to follow him despite life's adversity.
Jesus' body is composed of the living and dead!
In the end, Christians must come together as a family
To bring Jesus' message to all, so the world is fed
With hope and love, or we'll lie in our own beds,
Not in his kingdom, being unwisely led.

"*I pray for those who will believe*
    in me through their (the apostles') word,
that all may be one
as you, Father, are in me, and I am in
    you;
I pray that they may be [one] in us,
 that the
world may believe that you
    sent me." (John 17:20-21)

Christians! Joyfully accept Jesus' call;
Pick up your cross; follow him who died for all.
Don't be lethargic in your faith, lest you fall;
Complete the race and enter Heaven's radiant halls.

This story never ends! It goes on with you and those
whom you reach and influence. So show your love and
mercy to every one in every place by spreading Christ's
light to the whole human race.